Cambridge Elements

Elements in Politics and Society in East Asia
edited by
Erin Aeran Chung
Johns Hopkins University
Mary Alice Haddad
Wesleyan University
Benjamin L. Read
University of California, Santa Cruz

AUTHORITARIAN SURVIVAL AND LEADERSHIP SUCCESSION IN NORTH KOREA AND BEYOND

Edward Goldring
The University of Melbourne

Peter Ward
The Sejong Institute

Shaftesbury Road, Cambridge CB2 8EA, United Kingdom

One Liberty Plaza, 20th Floor, New York, NY 10006, USA

477 Williamstown Road, Port Melbourne, VIC 3207, Australia

314–321, 3rd Floor, Plot 3, Splendor Forum, Jasola District Centre, New Delhi – 110025, India

103 Penang Road, #05–06/07, Visioncrest Commercial, Singapore 238467

Cambridge University Press is part of Cambridge University Press & Assessment, a department of the University of Cambridge.

We share the University's mission to contribute to society through the pursuit of education, learning, and research at the highest international levels of excellence.

www.cambridge.org
Information on this title: www.cambridge.org/9781009572156

DOI: 10.1017/9781009572101

© Edward Goldring and Peter Ward 2025

This publication is in copyright. Subject to statutory exception and to the provisions of relevant collective licensing agreements, no reproduction of any part may take place without the written permission of Cambridge University Press & Assessment.

When citing this work, please include a reference to the DOI 10.1017/9781009572101

First published 2025

A catalogue record for this publication is available from the British Library

ISBN 978-1-009-57215-6 Hardback
ISBN 978-1-009-57213-2 Paperback
ISSN 2632-7368 (online)
ISSN 2632-735X (print)

Additional resources for this publication at www.cambridge.org/goldring-ward

Cambridge University Press & Assessment has no responsibility for the persistence or accuracy of URLs for external or third-party internet websites referred to in this publication and does not guarantee that any content on such websites is, or will remain, accurate or appropriate.

Authoritarian Survival and Leadership Succession in North Korea and Beyond

Elements in Politics and Society in East Asia

DOI: 10.1017/9781009572101
First published online: February 2025

Edward Goldring
The University of Melbourne

Peter Ward
The Sejong Institute

Author for correspondence: Peter Ward, pward89@sejong.org

Abstract: *Authoritarian Survival and Leadership Succession in North Korea and Beyond* examines how dictators manage elites to facilitate succession. Theoretically, it argues that personalistic incumbents facilitate the construction of a power base of elites from outside of their inner circle to help the successor govern once he comes to power. Then, once in office, successors consolidate power by initially relying on this power base to govern while marginalizing elites from their predecessor's inner circle before later targeting members of their own power base to further consolidate power. The Element presents evidence for these arguments from North Korea's two leadership transitions, leveraging original qualitative and quantitative evidence from inside North Korea. Comparative vignettes of succession in party-based China, Egypt's military regime, and monarchical Saudi Arabia demonstrate the theory's broader applicability. The Element contributes to research on comparative authoritarianism by highlighting how dictators use the noninstitutional tool of elite management to facilitate succession.

Keywords: succession, authoritarianism, North Korea, personalism, elite politics

© Edward Goldring and Peter Ward 2025

ISBNs: 9781009572156 (HB), 9781009572132 (PB), 9781009572101 (OC)
ISSNs: 2632-7368 (online), 2632-735X (print)

Contents

1 Introduction: The Challenge of Autocratic Leadership Succession   1

2 Theory: How Dictators Manage Elites to Facilitate Succession   8

3 The Kim Il Sung to Kim Jong Il Transition   20

4 The Kim Jong Il to Kim Jong Un Transition   32

5 Comparative Applications   50

6 Conclusion: Implications, Future Succession, and Further Research   58

References   64

An online appendix for this publication can be accessed at www.cambridge.org/goldring-ward

1 Introduction: The Challenge of Autocratic Leadership Succession

1.1 Research Question

Observers of North Korea have been fascinated by the sudden emergence of Kim Jong Un's daughter, Kim Ju Ae. First seen publicly in late 2022 (O'Carroll and Reddy 2022), her appearances alongside her father, especially at military-related events, have raised questions among long-time observers about whether Kim Jong Un is preparing for her to be his successor. If something happens to Kim Jong Un, who is only approaching middle age but is of questionable health (Cha and Katz 2023), Kim Ju Ae's young age (she is believed to have been born in 2013), and possibly her gender, could precipitate challenges if there were efforts to unify North Korea's top officials behind her leadership.[1]

Yet, while Kim Jong Un is the undisputed leader and most powerful individual in North Korea (McEachern 2019), it was also not certain that Kim would reach this point. When he succeeded his father in December 2011, long-time observers of North Korea similarly doubted whether he could survive in office, let alone consolidate power. For example, in a December 2011 *New York Times* op-ed entitled "China's Newest Province?," former Director for Asian Affairs at the National Security Council, Victor Cha (2011), wrote that whether North Korea "comes apart in the next few weeks or over several months, the regime will not be able to hold together after the untimely death of its leader."[2] As is true for all autocracies, the main threat to Kim at the time of his ascension was perceived to come from within the regime (Joo 2012). Elite splits are the biggest danger to any autocrat, either through leading directly to a coup or by motivating the people or foreign actors to challenge the dictator (O'Donnell and Schmitter 1986: 19; Svolik 2012: 4). This potential threat to Kim Jong Un was visible at his father's funeral, when the youthful Kim was accompanied by seven powerful men as he marched alongside his father's hearse. These individuals included his uncle and the rumored power behind the throne, Jang Song Thaek; the chief of general staff of the military, Ri Yong Ho; and the defense minister, Kim Yong Chun.[3] All had been key figures under Kim Jong Il, and

---

[1] The second of these points could also be a challenge for another possible successor, Kim Jong Un's sister, Kim Yo Jong (Cha and Katz 2023).
[2] Cha was not alone in this view; numerous experts predicted instability in North Korea following Kim Jong Il's death (Bennett and Lind 2011: 84; Byman and Lind 2010: 72; Gause 2011: 113; cf. Cumings 2012).
[3] Other figures included Kim Ki Nam (head of the party's Agitation and Propaganda Department), Choe Tae Bok (party secretary for international issues), Kim Jong Gak (head of the military's political officer corps), and U Dong Chuk (head of the country's secret police).

their experience, connections, and knowledge of the regime's inner workings predated Kim Jong Un's.

However, despite these men's more extensive experience of autocratic elite politics inside North Korea, the succession passed off peacefully. Accounts of the Kim Jong Il to Kim Jong Un succession point to the importance of strategic management of elites in allowing this to happen. For example, Kim Jong Il placed his brother-in-law, Jang Song Thaek, in key positions to help Kim Jong Un govern in his early years (Gause 2015: 46–54). Once in power, Kim Jong Un initially relied heavily on Jang to govern, but he discarded him in December 2013 by having him expelled from a Korean Workers' Party (KWP) politburo meeting and subsequently executed (Mansourov 2013). The case of how Jang was managed before and after the succession by Kim Jong Il and Kim Jong Un, respectively, highlights the importance of elite management for a succession to occur as planned.

Thus, although there is no guarantee that a transition to Kim Ju Ae would occur peacefully, North Korea has shown that even in the adverse circumstances posed by a young and inexperienced successor, the regime can pull off a peaceful leadership transition. North Korea's accomplishment is not unique. In post-Cold War Asia for instance, there have been successful autocratic leadership transitions in Cambodia (one), China (three), Indonesia (one), Kazakhstan (one), Lao (three), Malaysia (three), Myanmar (one), Singapore (two), Turkmenistan (two), Uzbekistan (one), and Vietnam (five).

The frequency of succession in autocracies around the world contrasts with academic research on the subject in two ways. First, succession has traditionally been viewed as a destabilizing time for autocracies (Herz 1952: 20–1; Huntington 1965: 396; Olson 1993: 572). Despite this, many autocracies in Asia and elsewhere have successfully navigated this supposedly challenging time. Second, there is a limited body of empirical research on the subject (Brownlee 2007; Frantz and Stein 2017; Kokkonen and Sundell 2014; Kokkonen et al. 2022; Kurrild-Klitgaard 2000; Meng 2020, 2021). We are therefore in the unsatisfactory position where succession is critical to the endurance of authoritarian regimes, but we have limited knowledge about how autocratic regimes carry out leadership transitions.

Empirical research on the subject provides some important evidence about how autocracies carry out successions, but our understanding is incomplete. Prior work mainly focuses on how autocrats use institutions to dissuade elites from challenging the incumbent when he is still in office (Brownlee 2007; Frantz and Stein 2017; Kokkonen and Sundell 2014; Kokkonen et al. 2022; Kurrild-Klitgaard 2000; Meng 2020: chap. 7, 2021). However, as the North Korea case shows, dictators also employ noninstitutional strategies to navigate succession. Further, as Kim Jong Il's and Kim Jong Un's management of Jang Song Thaek illustrates, elite management before *and* after the transition is important in shaping whether a succession occurs as planned. We therefore ask: How do dictators manage elites to facilitate succession?

1.2 Scope Conditions and Argument

In this Element, succession refers to the regular transfer of *de facto* leadership of an autocratic regime from the incumbent to another individual of the incumbent's choosing.[4] This captures a subset of successions in autocracies – regimes that lack meaningful contestation and participation (Dahl 1971) – but it is a significant subset. Dictators often attempt to hand power to their preferred individual, sometimes successfully as Kim Jong Il did to Kim Jong Un in 2011, and sometimes unsuccessfully such as when Egypt's Hosni Mubarak's attempt to hand power to his son, Gamal Mubarak, was interrupted by the Arab Spring. Other instances of this kind of succession include the transitions from Mao Zedong to Hua Guofeng in China in 1976, Nursultan Nazarbayev to Kassym-Jomart Tokayev in Kazakhstan in 2019, and Chiang Kai-shek to Chiang Ching-kuo in Taiwan in 1972. As these cases illustrate, this kind of succession can occur in any type of autocracy, and it can involve hereditary and nonhereditary transitions. There are other types of succession where leaders do not attempt to hand off power to a preferred successor, either due to a rare lack of interest (e.g., Castelo Branco to Costa e Silva in Brazil in 1967; Skidmore 1989: 40) or because they lack the power necessary to install their preferred choice (e.g., Hu Jintao to Xi Jinping in China in 2012). However, as noted, leadership transitions from one dictator to an individual of their choosing are a relatively frequent type of succession in autocracies around the world.

There are two periods when dictators pay close attention to how they manage elites to facilitate succession. Prior research on succession highlights the importance of what happens in the period leading to an autocratic leadership transition (Frantz and Stein 2017; Kokkonen and Sundell 2014; Kokkonen et al. 2022; Meng 2020: chap. 7, 2021). If incumbents fail to prepare or initiate a strategically flawed succession process, they risk elites attempting to remove them from office prior to their death or intended departure date. Thus, this prior work highlights that succession planning helps protect an incumbent from a coup attempt before he leaves office. But a corollary of these actions is that by deterring or resisting attempts to remove them from office, an incumbent's

---

[4] In contrast to irregular types of transitions such as coups, revolutions, or foreign intervention, regular refers to transitions occurring in accordance with the written and unwritten laws and norms of the polity.

actions before a succession also play an important role in allowing their successor to enter office. Then, research not explicitly on succession but on authoritarian survival highlights the importance of elite management for dictators once they enter office (Goldring and Matthews 2023, 2024; Sudduth 2017; Svolik 2012: chap. 3). To better understand how autocratic leadership transitions can occur, we therefore focus on (1) how outgoing autocrats and their successors manage elites prior to the transition and (2) how successors manage elites once they enter office.

Prior to a transition, we argue that incumbents prepare for succession by building a power base for the successor among elites who are outside of the incumbent's inner circle, or by creating the conditions that permit their successor to do this. No dictator rules alone; successors require a power base to stabilize the regime so that they can keep providing the functions of autocratic governance without disruption. Relying on incumbent-era elites for this power base, however, would be risky for the successor. These elites are comparatively strong, having spent significant time proximate to the regime's center of power. On the other hand, empowering elites who were outside the incumbent's inner circle negates this 'sovereign's dilemma' (Wang 2022) – when a coherent group of elites facilitates a strong state but threatens the leader's tenure – because the career trajectories of these elites become tied to the successor's rise. Elites who were outside the incumbent's inner circle but whose fortunes rise prior to the succession are likely to support the successor.

Then, after the transition, successors manage elites with the aim of consolidating the transition once they enter office. Looking to solidify their hold on power, successors seek to reduce the size of their ruling coalition. However, successors initially retain the elites who were raised in prominence to support the successor; these elites are valuable in helping them govern in the nascent stage of their rule. Successors do not retain these elites indefinitely though. Over time, they also marginalize these individuals to consolidate power and establish themselves as the regime's undisputed leader. Because our argument relies on an autocrat being able to manipulate the status of elites, it primarily applies to autocracies with personalistic incumbents.

1.3 The Evidence

We test the arguments using the two leadership transitions in North Korea from Kim Il Sung to Kim Jong Il in 1994 and from Kim Jong Il to Kim Jong Un in 2011. North Korea is rarely used to test theories about comparative authoritarianism with broader applicability – in this case, autocracies with personalistic incumbents – so why do we select these transitions?

First, North Korea features two leadership transitions from personalistic incumbents. North Korea therefore represents a typical case that we examine to probe whether the posited causal mechanisms function as expected. Failing to find evidence of the arguments would disconfirm our theory (Seawright and Gerring 2008: 299). Second, the transitions in North Korea represent prominent but puzzling cases of succession – prominent because of the value of understanding internal North Korean politics due to the regime's geopolitical importance and puzzling because many experts did not expect the regime to pull off either succession (Byman and Lind 2010). Third, the two transitions feature clearly identifiable periods before and after the successions where the outgoing and new leaders were attempting to prepare for and secure the succession. We therefore expect to observe evidence of our arguments in these periods. Relatedly, in the Kim Jong Il to Kim Jong Un transition, Kim Jong Il's stroke in August 2008 shocked him into preparing for succession (Gause 2011). This allows us to make causal inferences about how the second Kim's decision to prepare for succession affected his management of elites. In sum, examining the leadership transitions in North Korea entails explaining two substantively consequential transitions in East Asia and provides inferences about how succession occurs in autocracies with personalistic incumbents across the world.

North Korea has been largely excluded from studies on comparative authoritarianism not just because it is often viewed as atypical but because its opacity makes it hard to study. However, we utilize innovative qualitative and quantitative data to glean insights into elite management surrounding the transitions. For the Kim Il Sung to Kim Jong Il transition, we draw on a range of primarily qualitative literature, including elite North Korean defector memoirs, official North Korean government sources, third-country archival sources, and Korean- and English-language secondary literature. Then, for the Kim Jong Il to Kim Jong Un transition, we primarily rely on an original dataset of 1,953 leadership events in North Korea between 1994 and 2013, combined with novel biographical data on the 653 elites who attended these events. Dictators like the Kims use invitations to events to influence the power of elites; analyzing attendance patterns therefore provides insights into how dictators manipulate intra-elite power relations.

1.4 Contributions

The Element contributes to two bodies of literature. First, it contributes to research on comparative authoritarianism in several ways. Most broadly, we focus on an understudied but consequential topic – succession – and develop a novel set of theoretical arguments about how this process occurs. Research on authoritarian survival features many studies on how dictators avoid falling to irregular types of exits, especially at the hands of insider elites (e.g., De Bruin 2020) but also from the people (e.g., Chin et al. 2023) and foreign states (e.g., Escribà-Folch 2012). Yet succession is also an extremely common form of leadership transition in autocracies.[5] Several scholars recently investigated the determinants of peaceful succession (Kokkonen and Sundell 2014; Kokkonen et al. 2022; Meng 2020, 2021); however, to quote Meng (2020: 206), "[t]hough the politics of succession is considered to be one of the central challenges of autocratic rule, the mechanisms that facilitate peaceful leadership transitions are not well understood for modern dictatorships." This is partly because prior work focuses on how autocrats use institutions to facilitate succession. We therefore build on this work by highlighting a noninstitutional strategy that outgoing and incoming dictators rely on to stabilize their regime: elite management. Overall, by providing arguments and evidence of how dictators manage elites to facilitate succession, we contribute to knowledge about how autocratic regimes endure.

Then, we develop a new set of theoretical arguments about how autocratic leadership transitions occur by challenging a key assumption in comparative research about succession. This assumption contends that dictators do not care about the regime after their death (Meng 2020: 207; Shih 2022: 23).[6] However, Kim Il Sung's and Kim Jong Il's careful management of elites was not aimed at protecting their tenures from internal challenges but to aid their successors and support their legacies beyond their lifetimes. Case vignettes of elite management surrounding succession elsewhere suggest that this is a broader trend, which gives pause to consider how dictators' actions are motivated by goals beyond their political survival.

---

[5] There were 153 instances of leader succession between 1946 and 2012 (Chin et al. 2021; Geddes et al. 2014, 2018; Goemans et al. 2009). For comparison, there were 179 coups in autocracies in the same time frame (Chin et al. 2021); coups are a notable comparison because they are the most common irregular way that dictators leave office (Svolik 2012: 5).

[6] This may surprise readers since scholars sometimes write about autocrats' desires to perpetuate a legacy (e.g., Helms 2020: 337–8). However, this legacy is largely shaped by an autocrat's actions during their time in office, while leading scholars working explicitly on succession assume implicitly or explicitly that leaders do not care what happens after they die. Regarding the former, Kokkonen et al. (2022: 25–8) emphasize that primogeniture aids autocrats not because they believe their first-born male child is the best candidate for the job – a statistically unlikely scenario – but because appointing their offspring as successor helps protect them from a coup while they are still in power. More explicitly, Meng (2020: 207) writes that "dictators institutionalize their regimes not necessarily because they care about succession politics but in order to stabilize their own rule ... readers may have been wondering why a dictator would care about leadership succession if the transfer of power occurs after the leader has already died or left power."

Second, the Element contributes to North Korean studies. It first builds on but also challenges prior accounts of the two transitions. Many accounts of the Kim Il Sung to Kim Jong Il transition suggest that Kim Jong Il made few changes to the ruling elite during his first three years due to the precariousness of his position, with purges not starting until the late 1990s (Jeon 2000: 765–7). The Element challenges this narrative; drawing on new and previously untapped sources about the 1990s, we show that consequential changes to the composition of the ruling elite took place soon after and even before the transition – via the tactics of elite emasculation and purges – and this provided the roots of elite support that Kim Jong Il enjoyed throughout his rule. Regarding the Kim Jong Il to Kim Jong Un transition, observers agree that the party was important prior to the transition (Gause 2011), but we know little about how Kim Jong Il elevated party officials or how this aided a peaceful transition. As Gause (2011: 118) writes, "[h]ow Kim Chong-il [*sic*] secured the initial support for his chosen successor is not well known." We explain *how* Kim Jong Il used party elites to help ensure Kim Jong Un's position after the former's death. Then, post-succession, our account diverges from the main accounts of the transition, primarily by journalists or those in the policy community, which emphasize how attention-grabbing events, especially the 2013 execution of Jang Song Thaek, helped Kim Jong Un consolidate power (Fifield 2019). Instead, we contend that Kim consolidated power before purging Jang, through sidelining specific elites at certain times to implement a strategically sequenced process of selective marginalization.

The Element further contributes to North Korean studies by integrating the country more deeply within the study of comparative authoritarianism. North Korea has traditionally been viewed as an idiosyncratic autocracy and has largely been excluded from research on comparative authoritarianism.[7] However, scholars have recently demonstrated the applicability of comparative theory to explain North Korean politics (Koo et al. 2016; Mahdavi and Ishiyama 2020; McEachern 2018; Song and Wright 2018). We take this further, testing a set of comparative arguments using data from North Korea for primarily methodological reasons, and then demonstrating through comparative applications of the argument in other autocracies with personalistic incumbents that studying North Korean politics can help us learn about how autocracy functions in broader contexts.

1.5 Roadmap

The Element proceeds in five remaining sections. Section 2 provides the Element's theoretical arguments. We set out two main arguments about how dictators manage elites to facilitate succession. These focus on (1) how

---

[7] For exceptions, see Dukalskis (2021) and Gerschewski (2023).

autocrats manage elites to prepare for the transition to the incumbent's preferred successor and (2) how successors manage elites to consolidate power and solidify the transition. Since the arguments apply beyond North Korea, we set out these arguments in general comparative terms, with occasional illustrative examples from North Korea and broader personalistic authoritarian contexts.

Sections 3 and 4 test these arguments using the transitions in North Korea from Kim Il Sung to Kim Jong Il and Kim Jong Il to Kim Jong Un, respectively. Our use of empirical evidence in these sections is the inverse of one another. In Section 3, we adopt a primarily qualitative approach, drawing from a range of primary and secondary English- and Korean-language sources, including original North Korean sources, to identify how Kim Il Sung facilitated the construction of a power base for Kim Jong Il, and then how Kim Jong Il managed elites once he came to power. We supplement this qualitative analysis with some descriptive data on which elites attended public leadership events, subject to data availability. Then, in Section 4, we employ a primarily quantitative approach using an original dataset of 1,953 leadership events between 1994 and 2013, combined with novel biographical data on the 653 elites who attended these events. To gain insights into what is driving our quantitative findings, we supplement this quantitative analysis with qualitative insights of how Kim Jong Il and Kim Jong Un managed elites before and after the transition.

Section 5 moves beyond North Korea, providing comparative applications of the Element's arguments. As mentioned, our arguments primarily apply to autocracies with personalistic incumbents. Beyond this scope condition, however, we provide illustrative qualitative evidence that the arguments apply to autocracies irrespective of ideology, institutional makeup, and whether the succession is hereditary. We provide case vignettes of autocratic elite management surrounding succession in China's party-based regime, Egypt's military regime, and monarchical Saudi Arabia.

Section 6 concludes by considering implications of the findings for researchers and practitioners, what our findings suggest about how future succession in North Korea may occur, and questions for future research.

2 Theory: How Dictators Manage Elites to Facilitate Succession

2.1 Introduction

This section contains comparative theoretical arguments about how dictators manage elites to facilitate leadership succession. These arguments are causal in that we explain (a) how preparing for succession affects a personalistic dictator's management of elites and (b) how a successor attempting to solidify a transition affects elite management. We first posit that incumbents prepare for succession by building, or enabling the successor to build, a power base of elites from outside their inner circle to help the successor stabilize the regime once they come to power. Then, we describe how successors manage elites to solidify the transition, arguing that successors reduce the size of their ruling coalition to consolidate power. The exceptions to this are the elites who the preceding autocrat raised up in prominence to support the successor; successors initially retain these individuals because they can help them govern in the nascent stage of their rule.

2.2 Elite Management before Succession

A growing body of empirical research shows that incumbents use primarily institutional solutions to stabilize their regime against the future shadow of succession (Brownlee 2007; Frantz and Stein 2017; Kokkonen and Sundell 2014; Kokkonen et al. 2022; Kurrild-Klitgaard 2000; Meng 2020: chap. 7, 2021). These studies assess evidence from Europe and sub-Saharan Africa as well as a global sample of post-World War II non-monarchical regimes to explore how incumbents solve the thorny issue of succession. For example, examining forty-two European states between 1000 and 1800, Kokkonen and Sundell (2014) show that succession based on agnatic primogeniture – the oldest son inheriting power – reduces the likelihood of monarchs being deposed. This argument encapsulates the themes in these studies about how institutionalized rules can facilitate succession: They bring clarity and predictability to an otherwise unstable situation, thereby dissuading elites from challenging the incumbent.

However, incumbents care about succession for reasons beyond stabilizing their rule (Wong and Chan 2021: 595; cf. Meng 2020: 207, 2021: 958; Shih 2022: 23). If the incumbent has not died, a handpicked successor can protect the incumbent from arrest or execution after leaving office (Goemans 2008: 772). Incumbents also often care about protecting their family and allies after their departure, as well as preserving their legacy (Lachapelle et al. 2020: 35). For example, before succeeding Mahathir Mohamad in 2003, knowing it was important to Mahathir, Abdullah Badawi told him that "'My vision for Malaysia is Vision 2020,' which was Dr. Mahathir's blueprint" (Wain 2009: 307). For these reasons, incumbents do not just desire regime stability before the succession; they also want stability after they are gone and the successor takes over.

Incumbents therefore often seek to empower the successor for when he takes power, so that he can achieve the goals described in the previous paragraph. If the successor is not empowered, instability may ensue. Meng (2020: 208) observes that power vacuums after a leader's death can invite coups or civil war as elites fight to become the incumbent.[8] In a less extreme scenario, a successor may hold the position of *de jure* leader, but if they lack *de facto* power then challenges from elites are more likely because elites will see the successor as weak. A successor being weak can also precipitate agitation from actors outside the regime – that is, the people or a foreign state – who seek to capitalize on regime weakness (Bueno de Mesquita and Smith 2017; Kokkonen et al. 2022: 19). In short, successors experience instability when they are insufficiently empowered to govern effectively. Incumbents therefore seek to empower the successor so that he can stabilize the regime by continuing to provide the functions of autocratic governance. This subsequently helps the successor deter, or at least overcome, challenges within and outside the regime.

It is a well-known aphorism that no dictator governs alone (Svolik 2012: 79). Dictators require a power base of trusted elites who can help them nullify threats within the regime, control the people, and navigate threats from foreign states; these are the primary sources of threat to an autocrat's survival (Svolik 2012: 4–5). In North Korea, the regime's founding leader Kim Il Sung relied especially on elites who had fought alongside him as guerrillas in Manchuria during the Japanese occupation of the Korean Peninsula (Lankov 2013: chap. 1). A power base of trusted elites is essential for all dictators, including successors, to help them wield the 'infrastructural power' of the state. This is "the capacity of the state to actually penetrate civil society, and to implement logistically political decisions throughout the realm" (Mann 1984: 189). Put differently, dictators require support from elites to enforce their will across the polity, handling functions like repression, surveillance, propaganda, and other forms of political control necessary, thereby stabilizing the regime and ensuring the leader's continuing rule (Hassan et al. 2022).

Incumbents therefore prepare for succession by building a power base for their successor, or by creating the conditions for their successor to do so (Meng 2020: 309). This helps the successor, once in office, gain control of the state to govern and subsequently maintain power.[9] To emphasize, this power base is not intended to counterbalance incumbent-era elites or the military once the successor is in power (De Bruin 2020); although it helps the successor avoid falling to a coup, it does not do this via traditional means of coup-proofing (Quinlivan 1999). Rather, a power base helps the successor command the 'infrastructural power' of the state, helping the dictator harness the state's coercive apparatus to maintain control over the people and persuade incumbent-era elites to refrain

---

[8] See also Frantz and Stein (2017); Kokkonen et al. (2022).
[9] Meng (2021: 963) emphasizes the importance of elites supporting the successor, but while she focuses on how this helps successors come to power, we highlight the role elite support plays in empowering the successor so that he can govern and maintain power.

from obstruction (Gerschewski 2013: 21–2). Thus, a power base helps a successor avoid falling to a coup by helping the successor continue to deliver the functions of autocratic governance that are essential to the regime's stability.

Building a power base for the successor entails the earlier empowerment of elites who will make up this power base. These elites then have the necessary clout within the regime to enact the successor's directives. To empower elites, dictators often bestow prestigious tasks upon them, either through formal roles or by involving them in public displays of governance. These strategies signal an elite's importance within the regime and help them develop expertise. In Egypt, for example, before he was assassinated, Anwar Sadat prepared for succession to Hosni Mubarak (Time 1981). Key elites were empowered to establish a support base for Mubarak. This included Abu Ghazala, who gained valuable experience at dealing with the United States as the defense attaché to Washington between 1976 and 1979. Ghazala was then a key figure for Mubarak as defense minister from 1981 to 1989 (Springborg 1987: 6). The idea that dictators can empower elites has been noted in prior research. Kokkonen et al. (2022: 221) write that "[i]t seems as if the dictator is often able to decide how much to empower the elite." Building on this, not all elites are empowered to prepare for succession; instead, dictators empower specific elites to form a new power base for the successor to help him govern once in office.

In deciding which elites to tap for the successor's power base, incumbents and their successors must be careful not to trigger the 'sovereign's dilemma.' Yuhua Wang (2022: 13) describes how a "coherent elite helps the ruler strengthen the state, but threatens his survival." Wang's argument suggests that building a power base to strengthen the successor's grip over the state's 'infrastructural power' could strengthen the state but threaten the successor's survival. The power base for the successor therefore cannot be constructed from incumbent-era elites. These elites have garnered status and prominence via their presence in the regime's upper echelons of power and through their interactions with the incumbent. Incumbent-era elites have had the chance to develop important relationships with other prominent elites, as well as acquire significant material resources based on their proximity to the regime's center of power. Successors are generally not impotent when they arrive in office (Kokkonen et al. 2022: 114; Meng 2020: 209), but if they have to rely on incumbent-era elites, then they are vulnerable to being 'captured,' where elites force their preferences on the successor, or they may even be overthrown by these elites. When Park Chung-hee was assassinated in South Korea in 1979, his prime minister, Choi Kyu-ha, became president. Despite his former position, Choi was a career bureaucrat with no power base (Lee 1980: 70). In less than seven weeks, the powerful Park-era elite and head of the Military Security Command, Chun Doo-hwan, instigated a military coup to become South Korea's *de facto* leader (Kim and Larson 1988: 87).[10]

Incumbents and their successors therefore alleviate the 'sovereign's dilemma' by building the successor's power base from elites who are outside their inner circle. These elites are not nobodies; they could be deputy ministers in a party regime or princes in a monarchy who do not sit on the primary governing council. In Kim Jong Il's North Korea in 2008, examples include Kim's brother-in-law Jang Song Thaek, who was then not in Kim's good graces having been purged in 2004 (Ra 2019: 121–6), or the KWP official Pak To Chun, who had *only* been the party secretary for Chagang Province in the northwest since 2005; both became prominent once Kim started preparing for succession.[11] Regardless of their professional history or demographic characteristics, individuals chosen for the successor's power base are not members of the incumbent's inner circle when preparations for succession commence.

Building a power base of elites from outside of the incumbent's inner circle alleviates the 'sovereign's dilemma' for the successor (Wang 2022). The rapid elevation of these elites motivates them to support the successor for two reasons. First, elites brought into a power base from outside the incumbent's inner circle are motivated to help the successor govern and solidify his position because their rise in fortunes is indelibly linked to the successor's continued primacy (Weeks 2008: 41; York 2024). The removal or weakening of the successor would threaten the newfound fortunes of these elites.[12] Second, any challenge from these elites to the successor stands a low chance of success initially. These elites' newfound status in the regime's center of power means they have had little chance to develop strong vertical relationships with junior officials or strong horizontal relationships with fellow elites who might support them in a power grab (Goldring and Matthews 2023). Elites are unlikely to challenge the successor if they believe there is a low likelihood of success since the costs of a failed challenge are so high (Finer 1962). Thus, building a power base of elites from outside the incumbent's inner circle helps the successor wield the 'infrastructural power' of the state while not threatening the

---

[10] Meng (2021: 962–3) similarly discusses Félix Houphouët-Boigny's less-than-resounding endorsement of Konan Bédié in the Ivory Coast and the consequences this had six years later when he was removed by military figures with ties to Alassane Ouattara, Houphouët-Boigny's prime minister.

[11] Relatedly, see Shih (2022: 11–12).

[12] Cumings (2012: 216) writes that a Soviet official in Pyongyang chided Cumings in 1981 for focusing on Kim Jong Il's personality, saying, "Don't you know they have a bureaucratic bloc behind him? They all rise and fall with him."

successor's personal survival (Mann 1984), thereby circumventing the 'sovereign's dilemma' (Wang 2022).

This strategy is not without risks. First, empowering a successor who need not be the incumbent's son could trigger the 'crown-prince' problem, where the successor has the "motive and opportunity to mount a coup" (Kokkonen and Sundell 2014: 440; see also Herz 1952: 30). Second, increasing the size of the ruling coalition – a side effect of building a power base for the incumbent while not necessarily purging incumbent-era elites – could be dangerous since it decreases the value of membership of the ruling coalition; this is risky in autocracies because leaders engender loyalty through providing private goods (Bueno de Mesquita et al. 2003). Third, incumbent-era elites may react negatively if they believe they are being marginalized by the elevation of an alternative power base for the successor (Svolik 2012: 59). Elite infighting could destabilize the regime as a whole, potentially morphing into open conflict, even civil war (Roessler 2011).

However, there are logical reasons that explain why these possible costs are outweighed by the benefits of this strategy. Taking these points in turn, empowering a successor *could* trigger the 'crown-prince' problem, but this is unlikely for the same reason that certain institutional approaches tend not to. For example, Meng (2021: 952) describes how identifying a successor via constitutional rules mitigates the 'crown-prince' problem because, "once named, the designated successor has a strong incentive to protect the existing regime." The noninstitutional strategy of developing the successor's power base is similarly unlikely to trigger the 'crown-prince' problem because the successor knows that the incumbent is working to solidify their future. Then, contrary to the possible risks of a larger ruling coalition highlighted by selectorate theory, coup attempts are in fact less likely with larger ruling coalitions (Marcum and Brown 2016). This brings us to the related point that incumbent-era elites may react negatively to the emergence of an alternative power base. However, structural features of regimes with personalistic incumbents – the type of autocracy to which our argument applies – make this unlikely. Elites in these regimes have imperfect information about the dictator's goals and behaviors, including whether he is altering the intra-regime balance of power. This, combined with the risks of mounting a challenge, makes it costly for elites to try to stop the dictator. Personalistic dictators and their successors can therefore manipulate elites' statuses with a low risk of a challenge by incumbent-era elites (Svolik 2012: 55–60).

Incumbents and their successors sometimes also marginalize prominent elites while developing a power base for their successor, but whether they do this is conditional on perceptions of the dictator's strength among elites.

Marginalizing elites through purges may seem appealing, for instance, because it removes potential rivals to the successor; in Syria, Hafez al-Assad sought to secure Bashir al-Assad's succession in part by purging military elites who were opposed to the succession or had poor relations with Bashir (Leverett 2005: 62). However, purging elites can precipitate a backlash (Sudduth 2017). For example, Zimbabwe's Robert Mugabe was removed from office when he attempted to purge powerful elites to strengthen the position of his preferred successor (Beardsworth et al. 2019). Mugabe's old age and ill health signaled his impending departure and reduced the costs of challenging him (Bueno de Mesquita and Smith 2017). Thus, whether incumbents and their successors prepare for succession by also purging incumbent-era elites depends on the perceived strength of the dictator among elites. But even for dictators like Kim Jong Il, who was visibly weakened when preparing for succession, the structural conditions of personalistic autocracy mean that they can elevate a power base with a low risk of incumbent-era elites reacting negatively. For incumbent-era elites, being compelled to share the spotlight within the regime is considerably more palatable than being jailed or executed, the likely outcomes of a failed attempt to challenge the incumbent.

The argument that personalistic autocrats and their successors prepare for a transition by creating a power base for the successor builds on recent research on the determinants of succession. First, our claim that incumbents empower a successor echoes arguments about how institutions facilitate succession. Meng (2021: 953) argues that constitutional rules that identify the vice president as the successor increase stability before the transition "by empowering the designated successor." Second, prior work describes how successors undergo a grooming process (Kokkonen et al. 2022: 29, 114; Meng 2021). Analogously, by becoming more prominent and attaining greater status during preparations for succession, we argue that certain elites are also groomed to prepare them to become members of the successor's power base. Third, our claim that ruling coalition membership is likely to change prior to succession complements arguments about elite management around the time of succession. Scholars have described how the ruling coalition is likely to change once a new ruler succeeds (Kokkonen et al. 2022: 113; Svolik 2012: 198). We suggest that consequential changes in elite management also occur before the transition.

2.3 Elite Management Following Succession

We assume that successors wish to remain in power once they enter office, based on the broader assumption that all dictators wish to remain in power (Wintrobe 1998: 5). There are exceptions to this claim; Brazil's Castelo Branco, for instance, had no interest in being a dictator, but such cases are rare (Skidmore 1989: 40). The assumption also does not preclude the possibility that dictators have other goals, relating to specific policies or broader ideologies (Lachapelle et al. 2020). However, no leader, including autocrats, can accomplish wider aims without first maintaining power. We therefore explicitly assume that successors wish to remain in office.

The main threat to a successor's position once in office comes from elites who are part of the regime (Svolik 2012: 4–5). We assume that these elites wish to preserve their status within the regime that entitles them to private goods, whether through prestigious positions or direct financial payoffs (Bueno de Mesquita et al. 2003). The start of a successor's tenure is therefore a risky time for elites within the regime. Successors are generally inexperienced and untested at leading an autocratic polity (Leber et al. 2023). If their decision-making is poor or they convey an image of weakness, this could make the regime vulnerable to challenges. This could be via a regime change coup that overhauls the state's existing autocratic institutions or through pressure from the people or foreign states, which could herald the arrival of democracy. In any of these scenarios, elites in favorable positions under the existing autocratic regime would likely find themselves on the outside looking in. For instance, in the Ivory Coast, when Félix Houphouët-Boigny's successor, Konan Bédié, lost power to a regime change coup in 1999, his prime minister, Daniel Kablan Duncan, was not part of Robert Guéï's new regime and instead fled to France (CGTN 2023). Thus, elites who observe successors governing in a manner that they believe threatens the autocratic regime's continued existence might challenge the leader, calculating that the risks of perpetrating a leader reshuffling coup are worth the benefits of preserving their access to the regime's spoils.

Faced with potentially restive elites, successors need to solidify the transition, which entails establishing themselves as the unquestioned ruler in the eyes of elites within the regime. There are different ways that successors can achieve this. One seemingly appealing option is to institutionalize their regime. This means a successor accepting constraints on their actions and sharing power with elites, which generates a stable equilibrium (Meng 2020).[13] However, while institutionalization is an effective way for dictators to extend their tenure, doing so curtails their future freedom of action. Elites should not oppose institutionalization since it bestows greater power upon them, but they may oppose future deinstitutionalization, which is tricky for dictators to pursue thereafter because in the intervening time, elites will have been empowered by the preceding

---

[13] Institutionalization can involve, for instance, creating a legislative body that gives elites powers to participate in the regime's governance and subjects the leader to some scrutiny (Gandhi 2008).

institutionalization. Further, dictators who are strong upon entering office tend not to institutionalize, which implies that dictators prefer not to institutionalize when they have a choice (Meng 2020).

An alternative option for successors attempting to solidify the transition is they can seek to consolidate power. Consolidation refers to a leader having a significant share of power relative to elites within the regime (Gandhi and Sumner 2020). Consolidating power helps successors negate intra-regime perceptions of inexperience, unpreparedness, or weakness and reduce the likelihood of an internal challenge (Chin et al. 2022). Successors *may* arrive in office too weak to consolidate power (Leber et al. 2023), and so are compelled to pursue an institutionalization strategy to survive (Meng 2020). However, because successors are often favorably positioned by their predecessor in the manner described in Section 2.2 – that is, through the construction of a power base to help them govern as soon as they come to power – successors in fact have significant leeway to pursue alternative strategies, including attempting to consolidate power.

How, then, can successors consolidate power? Prior research highlights several institutional and structural factors that facilitate autocratic consolidation of power (Geddes et al. 2018: chap. 4; Leber et al. 2023; Timoneda 2020).[14] For instance, Fails (2020) shows that natural resources can aid consolidation by giving a dictator access to cash flows.[15] Dictators can buy the loyalty of elites and fund a surveillance state that deters potential elite conspiracies, shifting the balance of power in the dictator's favor. Alternatively, Leber et al. (2023) highlight the absence of oversight as critical to whether an autocrat can consolidate power. Specifically, the absence of old guard elites like the former leader increases the likelihood of consolidation. In sum, prior work highlights how structural and institutional characteristics, which dictators are passive experiencers of, affect whether they can consolidate power.

In addition to these factors, dictators have agency and can also proactively try to consolidate power. They can appoint officials to positions of high office, purge elites by jailing or executing them, and utilize various actions in between such as nonviolently dismissing or marginalizing an elite by excluding them

---

[14] Autocratic consolidation and personalism are technically different (Gandhi and Sumner 2020) but they are often defined and operationalized similarly by political scientists. For instance, Gandhi and Sumner (2020: 1546–7) define consolidation as dictators acquiring "so much power that they can no longer be credibly threatened by their allies," while Geddes et al. (2014: 319) define personalistic regimes as "autocracies in which discretion over policy and personnel are concentrated in the hands of one man." Due to the similarities in these definitions, we draw on research about both concepts to explain how successors manage elites to solidify the transition.

[15] Kim Jong Un similarly benefited from a resource windfall in the early 2010s. The price paid by China for North Korean coal rose from $80 in 2008 to above $100 in 2011, as Kim Jong Un was consolidating power (Jeong 2015: 14).

from certain events (Goldring and Matthews 2023; Shih et al. 2012). These tactics fall under the banner of elite management. Tools of elite management speak to the heart of autocratic consolidation since they directly affect the status of individual elites within the regime, which in turn affects the share of power that a dictator possesses relative to elites (Gandhi and Sumner 2020).

The question then, is how do successors manage elites in their regime to consolidate power? First, we contend that they shrink the size of their ruling coalition. Like autocrats in general, successors engender loyalty among key officials by providing private goods, which are more likely to encourage loyalty when there is a smaller number of officials because then finite resources are divided among a smaller number of recipients (Bueno de Mesquita et al. 2003). Engineering a smaller ruling coalition through marginalizing once-prominent elites allows successors to step out of the shadow of the former leader and other prominent individuals within the regime (Jiang et al. 2024; Leber et al. 2023). Decreasing the size of the ruling coalition therefore helps successors solidify their position as the accepted leader of the regime.

There are risks to this strategy, but they can be mitigated. First, larger ruling coalitions make coup attempts less likely, so diminishing the size of the ruling coalition could be risky (Marcum and Brown 2016). However, at this point a successor is focused on consolidating power rather than necessarily deterring coup attempts. Although coup attempts can be fatal for any dictator, they can counterintuitively help a successor because they provide an opportunity for the successor to identify disloyal elites and further consolidate power (Timoneda et al. 2023; Woldense 2022). Second, a smaller ruling coalition could also make a coup attempt more likely by leaving a small number of powerful officials remaining in the ruling coalition who could later perpetrate a leader reshuffling coup (Chin et al. 2021). But this risk can be alleviated if these elites can be trusted, which a significant proportion can be because they have been groomed for the successor's power base. Third, reducing the size of the ruling coalition could remove valuable expertise from the regime and make it more vulnerable to popular or foreign threats (Talmadge 2015). However, these threats are insignificant in contrast to elite threats (Svolik 2012: 4–5), so consolidation is a more pressing priority. Overall, the risks of reducing the size of the ruling coalition are surmountable and the benefits of consolidation and establishing themselves as the regime's accepted ruler make this strategy worth pursing for successors.

However, as noted, no dictator governs alone (Svolik 2012: 79). While successors reduce the size of the ruling coalition to consolidate power, they retain some officials to help them govern. They otherwise risk experiencing the fate of dictators like Francisco Macías Nguema in Equatorial Guinea who purged his regime to such an extent that there was barely anyone left to govern or protect him when his nephew, Teodoro Obiang Nguema, overthrew him (Decalo 1989). Since successors are trying to reduce the size of their ruling coalition, it is important that the officials they do retain are loyal. Private goods are intended to induce loyalty (Bueno de Mesquita et al. 2003), but successors are also strategic in who they select to retain so that these individuals do not take the resources that come with being a member of the ruling coalition and use them against the dictator.

Retaining loyal supporters is their primary concern but this consideration is challenging since loyalty is a latent trait and cannot be directly measured (Aaskoven and Nyrup 2021). Successors can use heuristics, however, to gauge the likelihood of an elite being loyal. This is a common strategy of dictators; for instance, in more ethnically diverse contexts than Korea, dictators sometimes use ethnicity to gauge expected loyalty (Hassan 2020). In the context of succession, recall how in the prior subsection we argued that preparations for succession involve the emergence of a power base for the successor. A successor reasonably expects that elites in this power base are more likely than other elites to be loyal. The sudden rise in prominence of these elites during preparations for succession intrinsically links these elites' statuses to the successor's continued primacy (Weeks 2008: 41; York 2024). Assuming they wish to retain this status, these elites are likely to follow the successor's orders, and they may even defend him if he is challenged. Thus, while successors work to generally reduce the size of their ruling coalition to consolidate power, they tend to retain the aforementioned elites in their power base to help them govern as they attempt to consolidate power.

However, successors do not retain the individuals from their initial power base indefinitely. As successors consolidate power, they eventually also marginalize these individuals. Although they are more likely to be loyal because they were raised up in prominence to support the successor, the timing of their ascent potentially threatens the dictator's status as the unequivocally most powerful individual in the regime. Since these elites' experience of top-level politics within the regime is similar to the successor's, there is a risk that these individuals may use their horizontal relationships with one another, their vertical relationships with junior officials, or their expertise at navigating the bureaucracy – which have all been enhanced by this stage – to outwit the successor (Goldring and Matthews 2023). These elites may not seek to remove the successor, but they can use their similar knowledge of the inner workings of the polity to influence policy, build personal fiefdoms, or even marginalize the successor. If he is to consolidate power, the successor cannot risk being seen as the 'first among equals' alongside these individuals; he needs to establish himself as the clear leader. Successors therefore need to eventually marginalize these individuals so that they can step out of their shadow (Jiang et al. 2024; Leber et al. 2023). Elites appointed to replace them, by contrast, lack these networks and independent power centers, being new in the job. What is more, witnessing what happens to their predecessor makes them more cautious and loyal. In North Korea, this risk was reportedly foreseen by Kim Jong Il. Kim Jong Un's uncle, Jang Song Thaek, was a key part of the power base developed by Kim Jong Il to help Kim Jong Un govern. However, Kim Jong Il supposedly also warned his sister and Jang's wife, Kim Kyong Hui, that "Jang's continued presence at the pinnacle of power would eventually threaten Kim family rule . . . Thus, from the onset of the Kim Jong-un era, Jang Song-taek's [sic] fate was not a matter of if, but a matter of when" (Gause 2015: 54). Overall, successors initially retain the elites raised up by predecessors to help them govern, but over time, as they consolidate power, they marginalize these individuals too so that they can become the undisputed leader of the regime.

This argument about how successors manage elites to solidify a transition makes several contributions to research on elite politics in dictatorships. First, our overall argument builds on recent work that highlights autocratic agency relating to power consolidation. Prior work largely highlights how structural and institutional factors affect whether dictators can consolidate power (Fails 2020; Geddes et al. 2018: chap. 4; Leber et al. 2023); instead, like Timoneda et al. (2023), we highlight that there are strategies that dictators can deploy to attempt to consolidate power. Second, our research helps further distinguish exactly why dictators reduce the size of their ruling coalition. Contrary to Bueno de Mesquita et al. (2003), Marcum and Brown (2016) show that a smaller coalition could heighten coup risk. On the other hand, we contend that if consolidation is the aim, a smaller ruling coalition is helpful and coup risk can be managed through careful selection of which elites are retained. Further, if dictators are confident that they can defeat a coup attempt, these are counterintuitively helpful for dictators trying to consolidate power (Timoneda et al. 2023). Third, while prior work raises the importance of elite management for autocratic power consolidation (Bueno de Mesquita et al. 2003; Geddes et al. 2018; Svolik 2012), our argument highlights the importance of target selection and the sequencing of when officials are marginalized. These are important factors to study to better comprehend the micro-dynamics of autocratic consolidation.

2.4 Conclusion

In this section, we provided theoretical arguments about how dictators manage elites to facilitate a leadership transition. This entailed first theorizing how personalistic incumbents and their successors manage elites to prepare for a transition, and then how successors manage elites to solidify a transition. We contended that preparations for succession involve building a power base of elites from outside the incumbent's inner circle to help the successor stabilize the regime once they come to power. We then argued that successors reduce the size of their ruling coalition to consolidate power. However, successors initially retain elites who their predecessor raised up in prominence to help them govern, but over time they also marginalize these elites so that they can step out of their shadow and become the undisputed most powerful individual within the regime. The next two sections test these arguments using the two leadership transitions in North Korea.

3 The Kim Il Sung to Kim Jong Il Transition

"Officials, if you should dream while asleep, you must dream of Kim Jong Il, and if you should work, every single piece of work you do must only be work that Kim Jong Il likes, and if you should walk, you must only go on the paths that Kim Jong Il directs you to."

"일군들은 잠을 자다가 꿈을 꾸어도 김정일 동지에 대한 꿈을 꾸어야 하고 일을 하나 하여도 김정일동지가 좋아하는 일을 하여야 하며 걸음을 걸어도 김정일동지가 가리키는 길로만 가야 합니다."

—Kim Il Sung, 1988[16]

3.1 Introduction

In this section, we assess the argument against the succession from Kim Il Sung to Kim Jong Il. We show that, per the theoretical expectations in Section 2, Kim Il Sung gave his son the scope and capacity to build a power base. Then, after Kim Il Sung's death, Kim Jong Il reduced the overall size of his support group, thinning it through emasculating officials. However, he did not marginalize everyone; he initially relied on members of his power base, who had risen in prominence between Kim being named the successor and coming to power, to govern.

We take a predominantly qualitative approach, using a wide range of sources, including North Korean defector memoirs, North Korean official sources, and secondary literature. We supplement this with quantitative descriptive data on leadership events, which provide another window into how elites were managed within the regime. Taken together, these diverse sources point to a new narrative

---

[16] Kim (2010: 10).

that emphasizes how proactive elite management strategies were crucial to Kim Jong Il's rise and his consolidation of power.[17]

3.2 Research Design

3.2.1 Background and Case Utility

In the 1960s, North Korea appeared to be just another Marxist-Leninist regime, albeit one whose leader had consolidated power. But in the mid 1970s, it became clear to some analysts that something unusual was taking place: the world's first hereditary succession in a communist country (Tertitskiy 2022b: 39). Yet, despite these seemingly idiosyncratic features of North Korea's first leadership transition, it has become something of a 'role model' that multiple authoritarian regimes have successfully emulated (e.g., Cambodia in 2023; Kazakhstan in 2019; Myanmar in 2011; Turkmenistan in 2022). Many aspects of the Kim Jong Il succession are thus far from unique or unusual to other autocracies with personalist incumbents. In Asia, an increasing number of dictators have and continue to anoint successors well ahead of the end of their lifespan in order to perpetuate the systems that they founded or inherited.

The Kim Il Sung to Kim Jong Il succession is a helpful case to explore how elite management facilitates succession. The clear and definitive designation by Kim Il Sung of Kim Jong Il as his successor allows us to identify how dictators prepare for succession. As we show in Section 5, other personalist incumbents employ similar elite management techniques to facilitate succession. The Kim Il Sung to Kim Jong Il transition is not just influential, then, but a useful case to examine to probe the causal mechanisms of our argument for the purpose of theory-testing because it represents a typical case of leadership transition in autocracies with personalistic incumbents (Seawright and Gerring 2008: 297).

3.2.2 Sources and Variables

We adopt a primarily qualitative approach but supplement it briefly with quantitative data. Qualitative sources are the best available to study elite management in the Kim Il Sung era. Sources on this period have dramatically improved since the 1970s when Kim Jong Il first emerged as his father's heir designate. There are memoirs from people who tutored Kim Jong Il, as well as from his sister-in-law, his son, more distant relatives, senior figures who spent time with him as a child and adult, and others who spent time with his

---

[17] In contrast, prior work focuses on generational change following natural deaths among North Korean elites being the main drive of changes in elite composition in Kim Jong Il's early years (Park et al. 2004; Kim 2009; Lee 2023).

half-brother. There are also accounts from people within the state who witnessed the emergence of the power base and Kim Jong Il's subsequent consolidation of power. Previously unreleased speeches from the North Korean leadership are also now available, some of which cover how Kim Il Sung supported his son's succession. Additionally, leaked North Korean sources provide useful insights into elite management under Kim Jong Il. We supplement these qualitative sources with quantitative data on leadership events. We only have such data for the Kim Jong Il era (i.e., from July 8, 1994), but these data corroborate a key insight about the post-succession consolidation period. We examine all these data through historical analysis, studying the processes underlying the creation of Kim Jong Il's power base during the Kim Il Sung era and the subsequent consolidation of power under Kim Jong Il (Mahoney 2004: 88).

The two main independent variables are when Kim Il Sung began preparing for succession and when Kim Jong Il sought to consolidate power after taking office. Kim Il Sung began the propaganda campaign to justify appointing Kim Jong Il as his successor in 1971, anointing him in private at the Eighth Plenum of the Fifth Central Committee (CC) of the KWP in February 1974. Kim Il Sung then publicly declared Kim Jong Il as the successor at the Sixth KWP Congress in October 1980 (Tertitskiy 2022b: 36–43). Thus, Kim Jong Il was appointed successor in 1974. We identify the actual succession as occurring following Kim Il Sung's death on July 8, 1994. Kim Jong Il shared some power with his father from the 1970s or 1980s (the exact date and degree of power are unclear), but ultimately his father remained the leader until his death (Cheong 2011). Then, to identify when Kim Jong Il was consolidating power, we focus on the period between July 8, 1994, and the turn of the millennium.[18] Traditionally, the consolidation of power by Kim Jong Il following the succession is dated to several key events: the end of the three-year mourning period for his father (July 8, 1997), his appointment to general secretary of the KWP (October 9, 1997), and amendments to the constitution that reformed the country's political institutions to make the National Defense Commission (NDC) the new supreme organ of state (September 5, 1998; Kim 2012: 2). However, we identify the consolidation process as finishing at the turn of the millennium since there were major purges in the late 1990s, which were tied to Kim Jong Il's consolidation of power.

The outcome of interest is the status of individual elites within North Korea. The management of these elites shapes the emergence, size, and membership of Kim Jong Il's power base. Autocrats have various tools at their disposal to affect

---

[18] Kim Jong Il's consolidation peaks later (2004) in Gandhi and Sumner's (2020) data on consolidation, but most of the increase occurs before 2000.

elites' statuses. They can purge elites, removing them from all positions that denote them as a member of the ruling coalition (Goldring and Matthews 2023); they can demote them from certain positions, even if the elite might retain others (Woldense and Kroeger 2024); they can increase or decrease the frequency and/ or importance of their contact with the leader (Goldring and Ward 2024); they can remove or confer on them important responsibilities (Woldense 2018); and they can promote them to prominent positions (Shih et al. 2012). The value of examining the statuses of elites through qualitative sources is that we can take a holistic approach, examining all these kinds of outcomes to track how the statuses of individual elites changed at different points in time in North Korea.

3.3 How Kim Il Sung Managed Elites to Prepare for Succession

Kim Il Sung was installed by the Soviet Union as North Korea's founding ruler, but it took time for him to transition the regime from an oligarchy to a personalist autocracy (Lankov 2005: chap. 1). Between 1953 and 1958, Kim Il Sung purged opponents in the party and military (Lankov 2005; Song and Wright 2018). The First Party Conference of March 1958 marks when all of Kim's major factional opponents were purged from the party and military (Buzo 2018: 46; Ward 2019). The last remnants of non-state farming and industry were also nationalized by 1958, which consolidated the party-state's grip on society (Scalapino and Lee 1972: 1060; Ward 2020: 79–80).

Kim thereafter built a state in which infrastructural power was concentrated in the party, as is the norm for communist states. Power was centralized in Kim's hands, through his position as general secretary of the KWP. The positions of minister of defense, minister of internal affairs, secretaries in the party secretariat, and major director positions in the CC apparatus were the principal conduits through which power was ultimately wielded. At the same time, Kim Il Sung was premier and head of the cabinet until 1972, hence the cabinet office was also significant until then in the power structure (Scalapino and Lee 1972). After 1958, Kim Il Sung ruled alongside his own faction (former guerrilla partisans from his time in Manchuria) and with the support of a growing technocratic elite (Hyun 2006: 60).

Succession was almost never mentioned in open-access North Korean press before 1980 (Tertitskiy 2022b), but the factional struggles of the mid 1950s were rooted in this issue. Specifically, North Korean elites observed Stalin's successors initiating a process of de-Stalinization. This led factional opponents of Kim to question his growing power (Lankov 2005; Szalontai 2005). However, Kim Il Sung did not seriously consider appointing a successor until after 1970 (Tertitskiy 2022b: 34).

Elite North Korean defector accounts indicate that Kim Jong Il was not designated as the successor in his youth, but he started being groomed for high office at university. He received bespoke lessons from members of his father's personal secretariat and from other members of the elite (Jung 2000: 90). Kim Yong Ju, his uncle and Kim Il Sung's brother, was particularly important in his education and acted as something akin to a guardian (Jung 2000: 91; Son 2004: 40).[19] Kim Jong Il also got the opportunity to listen in on cabinet, as well as meetings of the party CC, politburo, and military officials (Jung 2000: 93; Son 2004: 45). With his uncle's support, he also became actively involved in the management of Kim Il Sung University through its party committee (Son 2004: 45–6). These activities were early apprenticeships for high office, and thereafter, Kim Jong Il was given positions in the Organization and Guidance Department (OGD) and then the Agitation and Propaganda Department (APD) of the central party. Appointments to official positions and media messages are controlled by the OGD and the APD, respectively (Scalapino and Lee 1972: 740).[20] These roles therefore allowed him to build networks in two of the most powerful departments in the central party bureaucracy and of the entire party-state: (1) its human resources department (OGD) and (2) its public relations department (APD).

Kim Jong Il was confirmed as successor in 1974; his father then began openly supporting his policy initiatives and standing within the party state.[21] The organizational positions that Kim Il Sung bestowed on Kim Jong Il also allowed the latter to build up substantial personal power and a power base of supporters. Some of these individuals had been friends or allies for far longer. Unlike Kim

---

[19] Prior to the early 1970s, Kim Yong Ju was thought to be being groomed for succession (Hwang 1999: 168, 172–3; Jung 2000: 38). However, while Kim Il Sung's younger brother emerged as a major player in the mid 1960s, he was never designated successor. Rather, acting on behalf of his elder brother, Kim Yong Ju was instrumental in the rise of his nephew, Kim Jong Il. Kim Jong Il's stepmother, Kim Song Ae, also sought to have one of her children appointed successor, but she was outmaneuvered by Kim Jong Il with support from elites including Kim Yong Ju (Son 2004: 72–81). Kim Jong Il outmaneuvered Kim Song Ae through the support networks he had cultivated in the party with his father's support. For instance, Kim Jong Il used his position at the APD not only to strengthen his father's cult of personality but also to glorify his father's comrades-in-arms with the creation of revolutionary operas like *Sea of Blood* and *Flower Girl*, which were both well-received by them (Son 2004: 82; Jung 2000: 125). Perhaps the most powerful of these elites, Choe Hyon, defense minister (1968–76), then pushed for Kim Jong Il's appointment as successor at an informal meeting of party elders convoked by Kim Il Sung in 1972 (Son 2004: 82–3).

[20] Scalapino and Lee (1972: 740) note that in the Fourth Central Committee (1961–1970), eleven cadres in the CC had prior or current connections to the OGD, seven to the APD, and these cadres were generally higher up the CC list than average.

[21] Kim Il Sung supported his son's succession by endorsing his activities in speeches to mass audiences (Kim 2004: 187–8), confirming his son's control over party personnel management (Kim 2004: 213), making clear to officials that he received reports from his son daily (Kim 2005: 352), and requiring the permission of either himself or his son for criticism meetings of economic officials (Kim 2006: 464).

Jong Un after him, Kim Jong Il attended high school and university in the country and had a large network, which was used to staff the upper echelons of the security sector and the party. Kim utilized the powers of appointment he had through his control of the OGD, and his father largely deferred to his son's choices (Jung 2000: 123, 163).

Consequently, when preparations for succession were underway in the second half of the 1970s as well as the 1980s, a power base for Kim Jong Il began to form. Kim Jong Il cultivated an entire generation of future high-level party, state, and military officials. Some were close confidants he picked up post-1964, after he started working in the central party apparatus, others rose to prominence later. North Korea did not just become a hereditary dictatorship at the level of the leader but also among those who surrounded Kim Il Sung in the 1930s and 1940s. This second-generation group of elites emerged in the 1970s, and by the early 1990s, much, but not all, of Kim Il Sung's original group had died or retired (Hyun 2006: chap. 4; Lee 1992, 1995, 2000; Jung 2000, 240–52). Many of these elites achieved elevated status through connections to Kim Jong Il, while some were already at the lower echelons of the party-state bureaucracy when Kim Jong Il became the successor. Kim Jong Il did not pluck these officials from nowhere, but they were relative outsiders, junior officials with positions in the bureaucracy, which accorded them some power and resources that they could call on in his service.

With the support of his father, having created a group of loyal lieutenants in the OGD and the APD, Kim Jong Il then built a financial infrastructure of foreign trade enterprises (with large industrial and extractive affiliates) and banks under a new office, Office 39, staffed by loyalists to fund his emerging leadership (Kim 2008: 53–67). He also created his own secretariat that helped him coordinate and concentrate power (Hyun 2006: 142–3), and he established the Ministry of State Security (MSS), the country's secret police, as a new and separate state agency. The MSS fast became the most feared of agencies for its power to monitor and surveil the population, party officials, and elites for anti-system sentiments or conspiracies (Kwak 2018: 19–21). Kim made a close confident from the time, Ri Jin Su, the minister of state security. Another close elite, Sim Chang Hwal, was given the head position at the Ministry of Public Security's Political Bureau, the country's ordinary police, further enhancing Kim's control over society (Hyun 2006: 150).

Kim Jong Il's succession was publicly unveiled at the Sixth Party Congress in 1980.[22] The 1980s then saw substantial changes to the composition of the ruling

---

[22] Although our primary focus is on the relationships among elites within autocratic North Korea, the prominent coverage of this public pronouncement in North Korean media also helped legitimize Kim Jong Il's image as successor among the masses. As Dukalskis (2017: 15) writes,

elite; the CC was increasingly filled with people personally loyal to Kim Jong Il rather than those associated with his father's rule (Kim and Lee 2009). For instance, So Yun Sok, party chief for Pyongyang in the 1980s, joined the CC in 1980 alongside O Kuk Ryol (a key military elite), while Jon Pyong Ho (a munitions expert) did so in 1982. The 1980 CC was more than 70 percent new, though turnover was usually high in the Kim Il Sung era (Lee 1982: 443). Thus, the changes to the composition of North Korea's elite that were underway behind the scenes from 1974, which had increasingly populated North Korea's key institutions of governance in the party-state with Kim Jong Il's supporters, spread upward to the public-facing CC in the 1980s.

After the succession, the North Korean elite was increasingly dominated by the military; indeed, much of Kim Jong Il's public retinue were senior military personnel. Yet it was only in the early 1990s that Kim Jong Il began building an elite power base in the military, after his father appointed him as head of the Korean People's Army (KPA). Much of Kim's power base in the military was composed of close confidants who he worked with more closely after 1991 (Hyun 2006: 150, 156n247). But it is worth stressing that Kim Jong Il's power base was initially primarily more in the party, although in the early 1990s he built closer ties with members of the military beyond some of his father's more senior military confidants.

The evidence of how preparations occurred for the Kim Il Sung to Kim Jong Il transition highlights the difference between our argument and previous research about how autocrats prepare for succession. Prior comparative research highlights how incumbent autocrats use institutions, such as formal rules regarding succession, to prevent coup attempts against them once it becomes apparent that they will depart from office (Kokkonen and Sundell 2014; Meng 2021; see also Hummel 2020). The probability of a coup attempt against Kim Il Sung after he identified Kim Jong Il as successor in 1974 was low, but this does not mean Kim Il Sung was unconcerned by the possibility of one (Yi 2003). In fact, the opposite was true; the likelihood of a coup attempt against Kim Il Sung was low precisely *because* he was concerned by this possibility, a fear that was enhanced by watching elite fractures in China related to Mao's equivocation over succession (Jin 1999: 54–61). However, the empowerment of Kim Jong Il through the key positions in the APD and the OGD, and the cultivation of a key group of supporters within the party-state,

---

in totalitarian North Korea, "a heavily circumscribed public sphere in which a regime's legitimating messages receive disproportionate attention fosters resignation and acquiescence to the regime's rule, [and] makes it more difficult to imagine alternative political futures, and therefore contributes to authoritarian power."

was not designed to directly protect Kim Il Sung from a coup attempt. This was done to provide Kim Jong Il with the support to govern once he came to power.

Overall, with the support of his father, Kim built multiple pillars of a power base that encompassed the party, security services, and the military. In a country where the 'party decides,' having a tight grip on party personnel and Agitation and Propaganda was essential. Further, in a consolidated authoritarian state, secret police are essential to maintaining the state's infrastructural power over society. The same is the case for the military, a major threat to authoritarian regimes generally. Kim Jong Il was given the space, time, and support from his father to build a power base over decades, drawing upon networks he created within the major organizations of the party-state.

3.4 How Kim Jong Il Managed Elites to Consolidate the Transition

Kim Jong Il became North Korea's leader, after Kim Il Sung's death in 1994, amid domestic and foreign upheaval. On the domestic front, the country's food production and distribution system was collapsing, a huge issue by itself but one that also posed internal security problems for Kim Jong Il. With a famine about to engulf the country, Kim was forced to ask the outside world for aid, having refused to reform the country's economic system (Haggard and Noland 2007). At the same time, the country's major political and economic sponsor, the Soviet Union, had recently collapsed, and much of the country's imports subsequently disappeared (Eberstadt et al. 1995). The famine led to a breakdown in public order, with Kim complaining to officials in late 1996 that the country was reduced to "anarchy" because of the food crisis (Kim 1997: 311). This led to illegal internal migration within North Korea, as people moved around the country, leaving their homes and places of work without permission in search of food, straining systems of state surveillance (Kim 1997).

On the international scene, Kim came to power as the country was backing away from the brink of war with the United States. North Korea began pursuing nuclear technology in the 1950s, the country's nuclear scientists experimented with separating plutonium in the mid 1970s, and they undertook conventional explosive tests in the early 1980s to perfect trigger technology for use in nuclear weapons (Panda 2020). The North became a signatory to the Nuclear Non-Proliferation Treaty (NPT) in 1985 under pressure from Moscow but continued pursuing nuclear weapons to the point where the United States was close to attacking the country in June 1994 to prevent it from going nuclear (Wit et al. 2004). Ultimately, the two sides retreated from the brink and in late 1994 they signed the Agreed Framework, which committed North Korea to dismantling its plutonium production complex in return for light water reactors and political normalization with the United States (Lawrence 2020).

Amid this tumultuous backdrop of famine and a tense international situation without its former and principal patron, Kim Jong Il sought to consolidate power. He did not do this through explosive moments of internal upheaval; comparative research highlights how dictators use a victory over real or imagined coup attempts as an opportune moment to consolidate power (Timoneda et al. 2023). Though there was an alleged coup plot prior to the succession in 1992 – the Frunze academy incident – Kim consolidated power after 1994 through subtler but systematic tactics of elite management.[23]

First, Kim Jong Il reduced the size of North Korea's ruling coalition. Unlike his father, who appreciated official, large-scale meetings of senior officials to facilitate decision-making, Kim Jong Il preferred to rule through a small coterie of officials whom he frequently invited to on-the-spot guidance trips and secret parties (Hyun 2006; Park 2017; Son 2004).[24] This is visualized with descriptive data on the average number of attendees who attended leadership events in North Korea under Kim Jong Il.[25] Figure 1 shows that as soon as Kim Jong Il took power, the number of officials invited to leadership events shrunk drastically, going from more than ten officials on average at an event in July 1994 to less than five by 2000.

In practice, Kim Jong Il shrunk his ruling coalition through two means. The first, generational replacement, is a tactic that previous accounts of how Kim Jong Il consolidated power highlight (Jeon 2000; Kim 2009; Park et al. 2004). According to these narratives, Kim Jong Il took limited steps to try to consolidate power because he was wary of the power wielded by influential allies of his father, whose status stemmed from having fought alongside Kim Il Sung in Manchuria. For instance, O Jin U was part of Kim Il Sung's anti-Japanese

---

[23] The Frunze academy incident involved military elites and reportedly more than 20,000 soldiers linked to the Moscow Frunze Military Academy being arrested for displaying insufficient gratitude toward Kim Il Sung for the opportunities he had granted them (Ha 2014). There was also a major purge of the bureaucracy, the so-called Deepening Group Incident that began in 1997, which was part of a campaign to scapegoat officials for the famine, rather than the result of a coup attempt (Ra 2019: 112).

[24] Kim Jong Il was notorious for holding parties with his subordinates that involved copious amounts of alcohol and debauchery (involving so-called pleasure squad dancers; Sin 1996; Son 2004: part 4). This appears to be how he built and maintained relationships with his confidants and held discussions about national affairs and policy. According to Hwang Jang Yop, the KWP's ideology secretary before defecting, these parties led to a significant number of deaths from alcohol-related diseases and car accidents; the parties were too secret to involve drivers and high-level cadres sometimes crashed driving themselves home (Hwang, J. 2006: 311–12).

[25] We describe how these data were collected in Section 4.

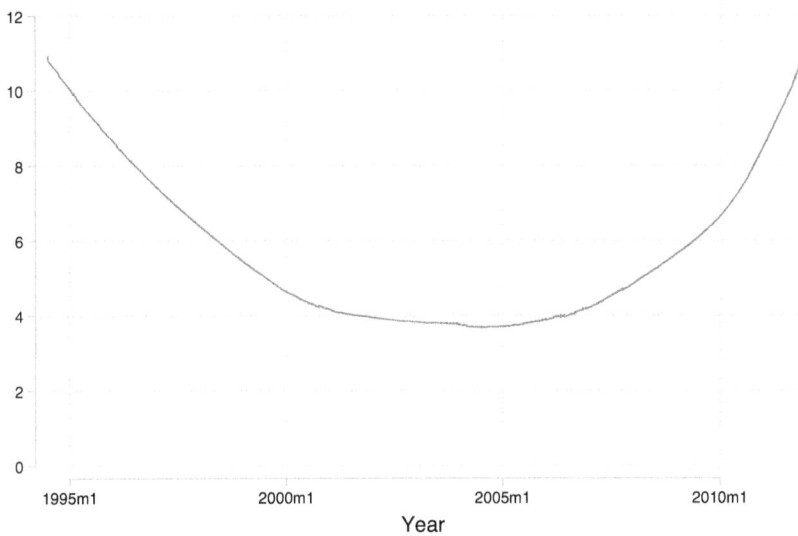

Figure 1 Lowess smoothed average number of elites at leadership events under Kim Jong Il, 1994–2011.

guerrilla activities in Manchuria. He was Minister of the People's Armed Forces from 1976 and was able to remain so until his death in 1995 (Kim 2009: 128). Overall, this body of scholarship describes how Kim Jong Il was only able to reactively shrink his ruling coalition to consolidate power when powerful elites died from natural causes.

However, Kim Jong Il systematically employed another subtler tool of elite management to effectively shrink his ruling coalition – that is, reduce the number of elites with notable power whose support he needed to rely on to maintain office – to consolidate power for himself. Specifically, Kim emasculated elites from the Kim Il Sung era, allowing them to retain official positions and roles that appeared to denote them with status, but concurrently he removed any substantial independent power from them by reallocating or diluting their responsibilities. Kim Jong Il applied this strategy to many incumbent elites from Kim Il Sung's inner circle. Elites like Pak Song Chol, Ri Jong Ok, Kim Chol Man, and Kim Yong Ju retained apparent high formal standing as members of the CC and sometimes the politburo but without actual power or real influence. These institutions increasingly became 'retirement homes' for old officials. What this meant in practice was that these institutions continued to exist on paper, and membership conferred privileges and prestige, but they ceased meeting and stopped being the institutions through which Kim Jong Il issued instructions or sought advice from (Lee 2023: 188).

However, Kim Jong Il did not emasculate all elites. As our theory predicts, he retained important figures in the power base that he built up with Kim Il Sung's support between 1974 and 1994 to help him govern in his early years. This included younger members of the Manchurian guerrilla faction, party officials from the departments that Kim Jong Il came up through (the APD and the OGD), and members of the security state. Among the Manchurian faction, several members of the so-called '1.5 generation' of former young guerrillas played key roles in helping Kim govern. Ri Ul Sol headed the KPA Bodyguard Command, a key counterbalancing institution, while Jo Myong Rok led the KPA Airforce and then the General Political Bureau under Kim Jong Il. Ri and Jo became members of Kim Jong Il's power base after he ascended to Supreme Commander of the Armed Forces in 1991 and became head of the NDC in 1993 (Hyun 2006: 150).[26] Many children of Manchurian guerrillas also helped Kim Jong Il gain a stranglehold over the regions, parts of the central party apparatus not under his direct control (such as the security organs, key heavy industries, and the youth league), and the military. Individuals who came up through the OGD and the APD with Kim held important positions across the state under his leadership, especially in party finance and espionage (Hyun 2006: 138–51), while Won Ung Hee headed the KPA's security command (its counterespionage branch) from 1989 to shortly before his death (Hwang, I. 2006); like Jo Myong Rok and Ri Ul Sol, Won became close to Kim Jong Il after Kim's elevation to head of the armed forces. Finally, several of Kim's family and relatives who gained key positions between 1974 and 1994 also become prominent figures after Kim's ascension. Most notably, Kim Kyong Hui and Jang Song Thaek, his sister and her husband, respectively, held various economic briefs in the party and key roles in the OGD in Kim Jong Il's early years. In short, Kim did not take a scythe to the entire North Korean elite after taking power. Instead, he strategically emasculated certain figures whose power or status derived solely from their association with Kim Il Sung, and to govern he relied on the individuals who had been cultivated into his power based once he was named successor in 1974.

Even these officials though were not safe indefinitely. Our theory suggests that once the successor has stabilized the regime, he should marginalize members of his power base since their prominence in the regime predates the successor taking power. Consistent with this logic, this is what happened in the late 1990s, once Kim Jong Il navigated the worst of the famine and his father's mourning period. Many members of the power base – younger members of the Manchurian

---

[26] Each was born in the late 1910s or 1920s and came of age supporting Kim Il Sung's Manchurian guerrilla struggle.

guerrilla faction, princelings, party officials from the OGD and APD, and members of the security state – were purged or marginalized and replaced by new individuals particularly from lower echelons of the military.[27] A significant portion of Manchurian guerrilla-related elites were purged in the late 1990s, including So Yun Sok and Ri Pong Won (Ri 2012: chap. 2; Yi 2003: 142). Choe Ryong Hae, the son of a key Manchurian guerrilla (Choe Hyon), was also purged on charges of corruption in 1998, after emerging as a key youth leader in Kim's early years (Jeong 2019).[28] From the '1.5 generation,' Lee Du Ik was also marginalized after 1998. Among the officials in Kim's power base who originated in the OGD and APD, many who subsequently held positions in the crucial security sector under Kim Jong Il were purged in the late 1990s. Kim Yong Ryong, the vice minister of state security, was executed in late 1997 (Paek 2005).[29] Kwon Hui Gyong, a senior official in the MSS and a key figure in the early stages of the nuclear program, latterly managed espionage directed toward South Korea, but he was also purged in early 1998 (Kim and Paek 2009). Even in Kim's family, no one was safe if they posed a possible threat to Kim's consolidation of power. In 2004, Kim purged his own brother-in-law, Jang Song Thaek, for allegedly undermining his authority (Ra 2019: 124).[30]

One alternative explanation for these purges is that they were driven by idiosyncratic factors. Each purge featured allegations of misconduct or the target being scapegoated: So Yun Sok and many others supposedly sabotaged the country's agricultural system triggering the famine of the 1990s; Ri Pong Won allegedly conspired against other elites; Choe Ryong Hae reportedly engaged in sexual impropriety and financial misconduct; Kim Yong Ryong was said to be in contact with South Korean spies; while Kwon Hui Gyong was allegedly insubordinate and corrupt (Jeong 2019; Kim and Paek 2009; Kwak 2018: 23; Ri 2012: chap. 2; Yi 2003: 142). Each

---

[27] For example, Hyon Chol Hae, the child of a Manchurian guerrilla fighter (Hyon Yong Taek), became the most prominent military elite of the Kim Jong Il era, occupying senior positions within the political officer corps after heading the KPA's rear services command (its logistics branch) in the 1980s (Choe 2023). Not all prominent figures under Kim in the 2000s were originally from the military though; Hwang Pyong So rose to prominence in the Party's OGD, while Pak Pong Ju emerged as premier in 2003 and played a key role in partially reforming North Korea's planned economy (Han 2009; Hyun 2006: 212).

[28] Choe Ryong Hae reemerged in the early 2000s and went on to play a key role in Kim Jong Un's early years.

[29] There is a possibility he committed suicide (Paek 2005).

[30] Kim had given Jang and his wife, Kim Kyong Hui, permission to use a guesthouse near Taesongho, a lake in South Pyongan province. Kim then invited a guest to stay there when Jang was away, but the guest was told by a guard that they could not enter without Jang's permission, which implied that Jang's authority mattered more than Kim's (Ra 2019: 124). Jang was purged but not executed; he returned from the cold in 2006 and went on to play a key role in Kim Jong Un's early years, before Kim Jong Un had him executed in December 2013 (Mansourov 2013).

case, however, highlights how power can be misused by elites in ways that undermine the dictator, thereby showing that Kim Jong Il needed to act to eliminate the perception of there being alternative independent power centers within the regime. Purges can serve multiple purposes, but overall, purges of elites in Kim Jong Il's power base helped him further consolidate power after having already emasculated his father's key allies.

3.5 Conclusion

In this section, we assessed our arguments using the Kim Il Sung to Kim Jong Il transition in North Korea. Utilizing a wide range of sources, including North Korean defector accounts, North Korean official sources, data from North Korean media, and secondary literature we have shown, first, how Kim Il Sung gave his son crucial positions and opportunities to develop a network of key contacts in the core organizations of the North Korean state, which gave him a power base that helped him govern in his early years. Second, the evidence shows how, once in office, Kim Jong Il shrunk the size of North Korea's ruling coalition through emasculating officials. To govern, Kim initially leaned heavily on the officials in the power base that he developed between 1974 and the early 1990s, but many of these officials were cast aside in the late 1990s as Kim further consolidated power.

4 The Kim Jong Il to Kim Jong Un Transition

"It is the height of fortune, pride, and luck for our party and people to put forth Comrade Kim Jong Un as the leader to succeed the cause of the 'Juche' revolution. Accepting Comrade Kim Jong Un is the decisive guarantee of all victories in this regard."	"김정은동지를 주체혁명위업을 계승해나갈 령도자로 내세운것은 우리 당과 인민의 더 없는 행운이고 자랑이며 영광입니다. 김정은동지를 잘 받들어나가는여기에 모든 승리의결정적 담보가 있습니다."
	—Kim Jong Il, 2011[31]

4.1 Introduction

We now test our arguments on the transition from Kim Jong Il to Kim Jong Un. Per Section 2, we expect that once Kim Jong Il started preparing for succession, he should have facilitated the development of a power base for Kim Jong Un. Then, in Kim Jong Un's early years, while we should observe him reducing the

---

[31] Kim, J. (2015: 425). *Juche* is "generally translated as self-reliance, meaning a withdrawal from the world economy and attempts at independent development" (Cumings 2012: 221).

overall size of his ruling coalition, he should initially retain the officials who Kim Jong Il raised up in prominence to help Kim Jong Un govern in his early years.

We adopt a primarily quantitative approach in this section, taking advantage of available data on leadership events in North Korea as well as biographical data on hundreds of North Korean elites in this more recent period. We present descriptive statistics and substantive findings from regression models in the main text but relegate much of the technical discussion to the Supplementary Materials to aid readability.[32] We also supplement the quantitative analyses with qualitative data on North Korean elite politics to illustrate the processes behind the statistical results.

4.2 Research Design

4.2.1 Background and Case Utility

In December 2011, it was already apparent that the transition from Kim Jong Il to Kim Jong Un was a hugely significant event in North Korean history. Although Kim Jong Il experienced severe health problems in August 2008, his death at the relatively young age of seventy surprised observers of North Korea (Tertitskiy 2024: 3–4). Kim Jong Il's premature passing also precipitated questions about whether his chosen successor and third youngest son, Kim Jong Un, would be able to successfully seize the reins of power and unify the regime behind his leadership (Bennett and Lind 2011: 84; Byman and Lind 2010: 72; Cha 2011; Gause 2011: 113). The significance of the transition also grew after it occurred because, as a second familial transition, it entrenched the Kim family as the 'natural' rulers of North Korea, something that was not widely accepted before the first transition.

The Kim Jong Il to Kim Jong Un transition is a useful case to examine how elite management facilitates succession from a comparative perspective. Despite Kim Jong Un's comparatively rapid ascension, like the Kim Il Sung to Kim Jong Il transition, there are many aspects of the second transition that are typical of leadership transitions in autocracies with personalistic incumbents; we return to this discussion in Section 5. The case is also helpful from a methodological perspective because idiosyncratic aspects of the transition permit increased confidence in the findings about how succession relates to elite management. As we summarize in Section 4.2.2, Kim Jong Il's health problems in August 2008 allows us to explore the effects of a dictator planning

---

[32] It is worth highlighting though that the quantitative data represent a significant empirical contribution to North Korean studies, which suffers from a lack of data availability.

for succession on ruling coalition management, while the post-transition period features a relatively clearly identifiable period when Kim Jong Un was consolidating power.

4.2.2 Sources and Variables

In this section, we employ an inverse approach to Section 3, relying primarily on quantitative data but supplementing it with qualitative data. The quantitative data that we use are attendance patterns at North Korean leadership events, which we drew on briefly in Section 3. These are public events attended by the dictator and usually one or more elites. They include on-the-spot guidance trips made by Kim – at anything from children's parks to shoe factories, or inspections of military units to missile tests – as well as major party, state, and military-related occasions. Data on events come from *NK Pro*, a platform run by *Korea Risk Group*, a leading media outlet on North Korea. *NK Pro* identifies which officials attended events from the North Korean state news agency, the *Korean Central News Agency*.

Leadership events provide insights into a dictator's preparations for succession because dictators can use invitations to events to manipulate the balance of power within the regime. Researchers have shown the utility of studying leadership events to identify which elites are in or out of favor (Haggard et al. 2014; Mahdavi and Ishiyama 2020). However, leadership events provide greater insights than this, in ways that can be informative when studying how a dictator prepares for succession. Dictators can use events to shape the dynamics of 'authoritarian power sharing' (Svolik 2012). Events indicate what policy the leader is prioritizing (Kim and Lee 2012; Lee 2002); an elite's appearance at an event therefore infers greater involvement in a policy priority of the leader. By inviting certain elites to events, the leader may not just signal but actively increase an elite's relative power. Similarly, by frequently disinviting an elite, a dictator demonstrates the elite's relative lack of importance to their fellow elites, or that the elite is being purged.[33] As Dale Herspring (1987: 43) writes about Mikhail Gorbachev's decision to invite only four military officers, down from nine in the previous year, to accompany the political leadership at a parade in 1986 to mark the anniversary of the 1917 October Revolution, "symbolic representations of power are very important; such things do not happen by accident." In systems where even for those within the regime identifying power is difficult, the perception of power becomes power (Schedler and Hoffman 2016: 97).[34]

---

[33] For example, former premier Park Pong Ju attended twenty-nine events in 2005, six in 2006, and was relieved from all positions in 2007.

[34] There are other ways to identify members of North Korea's ruling coalition, including using the membership of prominent institutions like the Central Committee (Kim 2021), but there are limitations to such approaches. Applying an institutional approach, for instance, can lead to time

Like Section 3, the two main independent variables are when Kim Jong Il began preparing for succession and when Kim Jong Un sought to consolidate power after taking office. First, we identify Kim Jong Il as preparing for succession between his stroke in August 2008 and his death on December 17, 2011. In most cases, the strategic interactions between a dictator and his ruling coalition represent a methodological barrier to assessing the effects of a dictator's actions on ruling coalition management. Put differently, it is usually difficult to assess whether, for instance, a dictator's decision to prepare for succession affects his management of elites or the behavior of elites leads a dictator to prepare for succession. However, the circumstances surrounding Kim's stroke make his decision to plan for succession plausibly exogenous to his relationships with elites in his ruling coalition. Kim's stroke shocked him into preparing for succession when he had not done so previously.[35] For instance, prior to 2008, Kim Jong Un did not receive any of the official titles and positions that would have enabled him to establish an independent power base. Thus, in plainspoken terms, because Kim's decision to prepare for succession was sparked not by his relationship with elites but by health concerns, comparing elite management in this period to the period prior to Kim's stroke provides clearer evidence about how preparing for succession affects elite management.

Second, to identify when Kim Jong Un was consolidating power, we examine the period between Kim Jong Il's death on December 17, 2011, and Jang Song Thaek's execution on December 12, 2013. Kim Jong Un came to power following his father's death. Kim's uncle, Jang Song Thaek, initially played a key role in supporting Kim. Once Kim came to power, Jang appeared to maintain his position as North Korea's *de facto* number two; some observers even contended that Jang was the real power behind the young leader (Shim and Tanenaka 2011). However, on December 8, 2013, Jang was relieved of all his positions and expelled from the KWP. Jang was executed on December 12, 2013. He was officially accused of engaging in "anti-party, counter-revolutionary factional acts" (KCNA 2013; Mansourov 2013). Jang's execution led North Korea watchers to reassess the

---

delays in identifying an elite's prominence or marginalization; positions are often awarded or taken away to confirm rather than change status. Using leadership events to identify members of North Korea's ruling coalition may not be a perfect strategy. For instance, prominent elites with secretive roles may rarely attend events, although even elites who work in opaque areas, such as nuclear weapons development (e.g., Jon Pyong Ho), still appear at events. In sum, leadership events provide useful insights about how the leader manipulates intra-elite power relations.

[35] Table A4.1 shows consensus on this point. Preparations were also never made for Kim's other children to succeed. The eldest, Kim Jong Nam, was exiled after being arrested at Tokyo's airport in 2001 for using a fake passport; he claimed he was visiting Disneyland. Kim's sushi chef from 1988 to 2001, Kenji Fujimoto (2003: 227–8), said the next eldest, Kim Jong Chol, was never the successor, while the youngest, Kim Yo Jong, is female and four years younger than Kim Jong Un.

balance of power within North Korea by December 2013. In short, Jang's execution was viewed as a clear sign that Kim had consolidated power to a reasonable degree (Gause 2015). Kim has consolidated power further since December 2013 – for example, the assassination of his half-brother, Kim Jong Nam, at Kuala Lumpur's airport in February 2017 removed a potential alternative ruler (Torkunov et al. 2022) – but he made significant progress to make the regime his own by December 2013.

The primary outcome of interest is again the status of individual elites within North Korea. Although we also use holistic qualitative data on elites' status, like in Section 3, we also focus on the quantitative indicator of whether an elite was invited to a leadership event. Under Kim Jong Il, the military official Hyon Chol Hae attended the most events (568 out of 1,573), and the 161 elites that comprise this sample, attended an average of 50 events each. Under Kim Jong Un, Choe Ryong Hae was the most frequent attendee (238 out of 380), and the 111 elites in this sample attended 19 events on average.[36]

4.3 How Kim Jong Il Managed Elites to Prepare for Succession

In North Korea under Kim Jong Il prior to 2008, military politics were dominant. The evidence in Section 3 showed that over time Kim began to purge or marginalize members of the power base that Kim Il Sung facilitated the creation of, including younger members of the Manchurian guerrilla faction, princelings, and party officials from the OGD and APD. Many of these were replaced by individuals from the lower echelons of the military. Thus, once Kim started preparing for succession after his stroke, military elites were more central in his inner circle. Wright's (2021) research on the structures of autocratic rule show how different latent features vary over time within a regime; in North Korea before 2008, this meant a tilt toward the military. This shift toward military elites in the ruling group occurred post-1991 as Kim Jong Il shifted his base of support as the country entered a period of crisis (famine). This was given an ideological basis with the 'Military First' (*Songun*, 선군) ideology. *Songun* meant that the NDC's power outstripped its purview in the North's 1998 revised constitution, and it became "the de facto general administration" (Gause 2011: 119). This was also reflected in the relative status of military elites within Kim's

---

[36] The Supplementary Materials contain details of how we identify the samples of possible elite invitees to leadership events. This most closely builds on data contributions in prior work by Kim (2021) who identifies whether 367 North Korean elites between 1948 and 2019 were in the KWP politburo, and whether an elite built their career outside the KWP, government, or KPA; Haggard et al. (2014) track membership of the secretariat, the NDC, and the politburo between 1994 and 2013; while Ishiyama (2014) categorizes thirty North Korean elites between 1997 and 2011 based on their political orientation as conservative, open, or moderate.

inner circle. For instance, elites in the KPA were Kim's "favored bodyguard" (Jeon 2009: 197).

Consistent with the prominence of military elites prior to Kim's stroke, once Kim started preparing for succession after August 2008, it initially appeared as though the military, especially the KPA, would be the foundation for the succession. Indeed, actions were taken after Kim's stroke to boost Kim Jong Un's standing within the military. A propaganda campaign in the military from December 2008 preceded Kim Jong Un being named a four-star general by April 2009 (Cheong 2010: 169; H. Kim 2015: 179; Thae 2018: 277). Members of the security services, including the military, were required to swear allegiance to Kim Jong Un in early 2009. Then, in the latter half of 2009, heads of the military's General Political Bureau and other security institutions began reporting to Kim Jong Un (Cheong 2010: 171). Kim Jong Un is also believed to have overseen several military actions to test whether the military would respond to him. The sinking in March 2010 of the *Cheonan*, a South Korean warship, and the November 2010 shelling of South Korea's Yeonpyeong Island are thought to have been ordered by Kim Jong Un in part to quiet voices of discontent about the succession and ensure that the military would obey him (Gause 2011: 167, 2015: 165n357; Haggard et al. 2014: 776; H. Kim 2015: 176; Shin 2018: 200; Shin 2020: 57–66).

However, Kim Jong Il's efforts to prepare for succession are closely linked to the resurgence of KWP officials. The KWP subsequently became the main institutional vehicle through which Kim Jong Un's legitimacy flowed. KWP cadres increasingly occupied prominent positions in important KPA and KWP bodies including the Central Military Commission, NDC, and the politburo. This helped extend Kim Jong Un's influence over the country's then primary institutions (Gause 2011: chap. 6; Haggard et al. 2014).

In contrast to military elites, party officials were relatively outside of Kim Jong Il's inner circle before his stroke.[37] Kim relied on some KWP elites prior to August 2008, including his sister Kim Kyong Hui, but KWP elites were generally not as close as military elites to the regime's center of power. For example, all the personnel sitting on the NDC in 2003 were connected to the military. After Kim's stroke, however, several KWP officials became members of the NDC (Haggard et al. 2014: 783–4). Our theory suggests that when preparing for succession, Kim should have integrated elites from outside his

---

[37] To be clear, all elites in our dataset are KWP members. But there is a difference between, for instance, being a KWP member and the minister of the armed forces versus being a KWP member and a party secretary. The former is a military elite, the latter a party elite. The Supplementary Materials describe how we identify the primary roles (in the cabinet, military, or party) that different elites have at a given point in time.

Table 1 Differences in means for the proportion of events attended by different types of elites.

	Cabinet	Military	Party
Pre-stroke	1.48	6.59	2.77
Post-stroke	2.77	5.61	7.19
Difference in means	1.30	−0.97	4.42*

Note: *$p < 0.01$

inner circle into the ruling coalition to build a power base for Kim Jong Un. This is precisely what we observe in the leadership event data, based on identifying party elites as generally being outside of Kim's inner circle prior to August 2008. Table 1 shows differences in the means of the proportion of events that different elites attended before and after Kim's stroke. Consistent with the theory, KWP elites attended 2.77 percent of events on average before Kim's stroke, and 7.19 percent after. This change is significant at the 99 percent confidence level. Further analysis that accounts for various alternative explanations suggests that party elites were 70.58 percent more likely to attend a leadership event after Kim's stroke than they were before.[38]

The increased presence of party elites at leadership events reflects systematic changes in the substantive importance of these elites' roles who, in general, were previously outside of Kim Jong Il's inner circle. Senior officials entrusted with managing party finances, party control of the military, party control of the military industrial complex (and nuclear program specifically), party work in the capital, human resource issues for both the elite and lower-level cadres, and officials tasked with political oversight of the security services became especially prominent. For example, Han Kwang Sang, who oversaw KWP finances, a crucial role as the party started to take greater control over KPA finances during this period, was regularly invited by Kim Jong Il to events in 2010 (four) and 2011 (eight), despite having never previously been invited. Another example is the rise of Kim Chang Sop, who was head of the political bureau within the Ministry of State Security (the political police). Kim Jong Il also suddenly started inviting Kim Chang Sop to events in 2010 (three) and 2011 (twenty-one), despite his previous absence. These elites are illustrative of the broader trend of party elites, who were previously outside of Kim Jong Il's inner circle, being raised up in prominence after Kim Jong Il's stroke and going on, as

---

[38] The Supplementary Materials provide details of the regression models that we estimated, as well as the robustness checks including placebo tests, which provide evidence for this finding. Details of these analyses are also in Goldring and Ward (2024).

we describe in Section 4.4, to play key roles in Kim Jong Un's inner circle in his early years.

Our theory also contains an implication for how Kim Jong Il should have managed military elites after his stroke. We posited that incumbents preparing for succession do not purge elites in their inner circle if the incumbent is visibly weakened, generally due to ill health or old age, when preparing for succession. Kim was visibly weakened by his stroke in August 2008. He therefore should not have attempted to overtly undermine the status of military elites, who we identified as the key elites in his inner circle when he started preparing for succession. Consistent with this, the difference in means (in Table 1) for military (and cabinet) officials is smaller and not statistically significant. Further analysis via regression models provides additional support for this finding.[39]

Thus, alongside the rise of KWP officials, KPA officers remained prominent in elite circles. Many combat field officers tasked with leadership roles, as well as the political officer corps, remained a key element in the ruling coalition. As such, many KPA officers continued to be invited to military and nonmilitary events, likely to provide feedback on policies or ideas for new initiatives. These included senior military men like Kim Yong Chun (defense minister from February 2009 to April 2012), Hyon Chol Hae (head of the Political Bureau of the National Defense Commission from May 2010 to April 2012), and Kim Jong Gak (first deputy director of the KPA General Political Bureau from February 2009 to April 2012). There were also some prominent new faces like Ri Yong Ho (the former head of Pyongyang's capital defense command who became chief of general staff (February 2009 to July 2012), and Kim Won Hong (head of the KPA security command from September 2003 to February 2010 and deputy director of the KPA General Political Bureau from February 2010 to April 2012). Nonetheless, these officers were associated with Kim Jong Il's base of power and were less important in providing a power base to help Kim Jong Un stabilize the regime.

One alternative explanation for the rise and enduring prominence of KWP elites between August 2008 and December 2013 is that Kim Jong Il wanted to focus on policies that KWP elites could help with before his death,[40] and then there was relative stasis in elite turnover while Kim Jong Un found his feet early in his tenure. However, KWP elites were not just more likely to attend events in general after Kim Jong Il's stroke; they were also more likely to attend military events specifically.[41] The argument that Kim Jong Il increasingly invited KWP

---

[39] See the Supplementary Materials.
[40] We thank Cheong Seong-chang, director of the Center for Korean Peninsula Strategy at the Sejong Institute, for suggesting this possibility.
[41] See Figure A4.8.

elites to events after his stroke because he wanted to focus on policies that KWP elites could help with does not explain the increasingly likely attendance of KWP elites at military events after Kim's stroke. Further, Kim Jong Un purged a high-profile military elite – Ri Yong Ho – in July 2012 (Gause 2015: 28). It is generally easier to purge civilian than military elites (Goldring and Matthews 2024); thus, if Kim Jong Un was willing to purge military elites, then it is unlikely that Kim Jong Un kept around party elites, whose prominence increased after Kim Jong Il's stroke, only because he was less sure of his position in his early days.

Another alternative possibility is that KWP elites became more prominent between 2008 and 2011 because Kim Jong Il was guarding against a military coup when he was visibly vulnerable after his stroke (Bueno de Mesquita and Smith 2017). However, there are several reasons to doubt this explanation. First, Kim Jong Il did not invite party elites more frequently after his stroke to expand the size of the ruling coalition and enhance the visibility of a formal institution – in this case, the KWP – to signal strong support (Timoneda 2020); the findings are robust to accounting for the number of elites invited to an event.[42] Second, the type of elites more frequently invited did not increase coordination costs for would-be conspirators (De Bruin 2020: 20–2; Matthews 2022: 667). Inviting KWP elites to events more frequently would not affect coordination costs since military elites could plot at other locations away from the prying eyes of KWP officials. Existing coup-proofing measures also already make a coup attempt unlikely. The military has a split chain of command, which inhibits large troop movements without consent coming from multiple sources. Leadership of the defense of Pyongyang and the leader's bodyguard are also both run separately and distinctly from the regular military chain of command (Ko 2007: 123; Oh 2012: 129–30). The embedding of political officers and security command officers (from North Korea's internal military secret police) within the military also makes a coup attempt unlikely (Tertitskiy 2022a). Kim purged some civilian elites after his stroke – notably the party finance director Pak Nam Gi – but there was little reshuffling of military personnel or military elite purges, both of which we would expect if Kim had been coup-proofing (Park 2011).

Overall, elites who were outside Kim Jong Il's inner circle before his stroke – KWP elites – became more prominent once Kim started preparing for succession. This evidence is consistent with our argument's logic – that this was to facilitate the construction of a power base for Kim Jong Un to help the younger Kim stabilize the regime once in power – and there are reasons to doubt the plausible alternative explanations for the quantitative findings. In the following

---

[42] See Figure A4.9.

section, we provide additional qualitative evidence from Kim Jong Un's tenure that is consistent with the idea that Kim Jong Il was facilitating the construction of a power base for Kim Jong Un.

4.4 How Kim Jong Un Managed Elites to Consolidate the Transition

Kim Jong Un's tenure as North Korea's leader began on December 17, 2011, when Kim Jong Il died. The global context was not as dangerous as when his father came to power in 1994, following the collapse of the country's major sponsor (the Soviet Union). However, Kim Jong Un still had to reckon with a moribund economy, extensive sanctions, and a thriving South Korea that all too many North Koreans were increasingly aware was not the capitalist failure that North Korean propaganda claimed. Additionally, Kim Jong Un came to power at the tender age of twenty-seven, after going through an accelerated grooming process since August 2008 to prepare him for succession. As we have seen, many outside observers doubted that he possessed the leadership skills or experience to be accepted as the leader by North Korea's elites (Bennett and Lind 2011: 84; Byman and Lind 2010: 72; Cha 2011; Gause 2011: 113).

Against this context, Kim Jong Un sought to consolidate power. The December 2013 purge of his uncle, Jang Song Thaek, is often held up as evidence of Kim consolidating power. But, as discussed, Kim's ability to do this indicated that he had already made significant progress toward this goal. Kim sought to consolidate power not just through the headline-grabbing tactic of violent purges but through the more subtle tactic of gradually reducing the size of his ruling coalition. This was not immediately evident because Kim Jong Un, unlike his father, sought to restore the primary decision-making bodies of the KWP, including the politburo, CC, and even the party congresses (Park 2017: 113–21).[43] However, over Kim Jong Un's first two years, there was a substantial thinning of the ranks. In a system where, as discussed, face time with the leader confers power, elites were invited less often to events in the build-up to Jang's purge, and Kim relied increasingly on a small coterie of advisers from the KPA – Hyon Chol Hae (First Vice Minister of People's Armed Forces from April 2012); Ri Myong Su (Minister of Public Security from April 2011 to February 2013); Kim Jong Gak (Minister of People's Armed Forces up to November 2012); and Jang Jong Nam (KPA First Division Chief in December

---

[43] Under Kim Jong Il, the politburo did not meet once between 1994 and 2010, while no party congresses had been called since 1980 (even though they were supposed to be called at regular intervals), and the Central Committee had also ceased to meet. Kim Jong Un revived these institutions, holding regular politburo meetings, central committee plenums, and even began regular party congresses (holding one in 2016 and another in 2021).

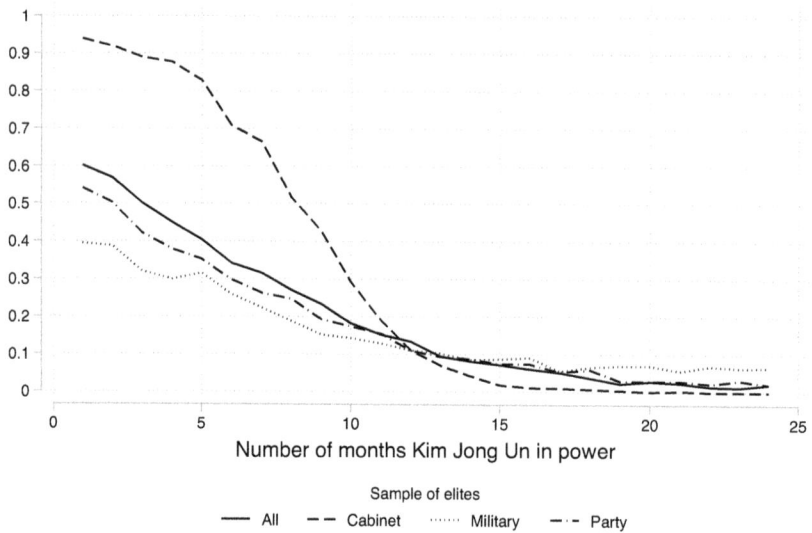

Figure 2 The probabilities of different types of elites attending an event under Kim Jong Un, December 2011 to December 2013.

2012, Minister of People's Armed Forces from May 2013 to June 2014) – and the KWP – Hwang Pyong So (OGD Vice Director); Pak Thae Song (Party Central Committee Department Vice Chair); and Ma Won Chun (Party Central Committee Department Vice Chair).

Kim Jong Un's efforts to reduce the size of his ruling coalition and consolidate power are reflected in attendance patterns at leadership events between December 2011 and December 2013. Figure 2 shows the probabilities of all elites, as well as different types of elites, being invited to a leadership event over Kim Jong Un's first two years in power.[44] Figure 2 shows that in Kim's first month in office (December 2011), an elite had a probability of 0.6 of being invited to a leadership event. This was just over 0.1 a year later, and one further year later it was less than 0.05. This reflects the emergence of Kim Jong Un's 'kitchen cabinet' of close advisors, like that which Kim Jong Il relied on (Park 2017: 108–13).

Findings from regression models suggest that the consolidation of power and corresponding shrinking of Kim Jong Un's ruling coalition in his first two years applies to cabinet and party elites, but possibly not military elites.[45] However, it is worth noting that, although data from South Korea's Ministry of Unification

---

[44] The Supplementary Materials contain details of the models estimated along with various robustness tests.

[45] We highlight this because the coefficient for a model based on the subsample of military elites is in the expected negative direction but is not statistically significant.

(MOU) shows that between the end of 2011 and the end of 2013 only 1.34 percent (21 out of 1,564) of one- to four-star generals lost their position, there were important changes to the composition of military elites (MOU 2011: 215–25, 2013: 227–36). Ri Yong Ho, the chief of the general staff, was purged (reportedly executed) in July 2012, the minister of defense was changed multiple times, a small number of other generals were demoted or lost their jobs, some major positions were subject to frequent change, and some senior, old military officials retired (Kim, T. 2015: 151, 153, 170). Thus, Kim may have been careful to keep the military on side, but he also sought to reduce the military's influence, including over foreign trade assets.

Like his father though, Kim Jong Un did not marginalize all elites in his first two years. Consistent with the theory in Section 2, Kim Jong Un initially leaned on the elites who Kim Jong Il raised up to help Kim Jong Un govern. More specifically, the majority of KWP elites who Kim Jong Il raised in prominence played important roles in helping Kim Jong Un govern between 2011 and 2013, unlike KWP elites who Kim Jong Il did not raise up in prominence.[46] They carried out key tasks to help Kim Jong Un monitor elites, control the army, and subdue the people. Table 2 summarizes the primary roles that KWP elites, who were raised in prominence by Kim Jong Il after his stroke, held in Kim Jong Un's early years.[47] To monitor other elites, Kim Kyong Ok was the first vice director of the OGD from 2008, a position he continued to hold in Kim Jong Un's early years. The OGD manages KWP human resource issues, including appointments, promotions, and disciplinary procedures (see Section 3). To quell potential threats from elites more broadly, Choe Ryong Hae and O Kuk Ryol helped provide control of the army, through their respective roles as chief of the KPA's General Political Bureau and vice chair of the NDC. Several elites also played key roles in the development of

---

[46] This is also evidence of the argument in the first half of the section. One additional implication of the earlier argument – that Kim Jong Il raised up KWP elites to facilitate the construction of a power base for Kim Jong Un to help the younger Kim stabilize the regime once in power – is that KWP elites who became more prominent should have played important roles in helping Kim Jong Un govern in his early years. Kim Jong Il coordinated succession plans with family members prior to his death (Gause 2015: 54), so if Kim brought KWP elites into his inner circle to build a power base for Kim Jong Un, we should expect Kim Jong Un to have governed, at least initially, by leaning on these elites for support. Finding evidence that these KWP elites helped Kim Jong Un stabilize the regime in his early years would affirm our argument's plausibility (Collier 2011: 825). We would doubt our argument's logic if Kim Jong Un marginalized these elites immediately after taking power. As we show here, KWP elites who were prominent under Kim Jong Il after the latter's stroke were more likely to attend an event early on under Kim Jong Un and played more substantive roles in governance.

[47] These are the thirty KWP elites who were statistically significantly more likely to attend an event after Kim Jong Il's stroke. We compare these in Table 3 with the forty-one KWP elites who were not more likely to attend an event after Kim Jong Il's stroke.

Table 2 Careers of KWP elites who were raised in prominence by Kim Jong Il after his stroke, December 2011 to December 2013.

Played important role in Kim Jong Un's inner circle	Purged or retired under Kim Jong Il
1. Choe Ryong Hae *KPA General Political Bureau Chief, April 2012 to April 2014* 2. Choe Thae Bok *KWP Secretary for Education, 1993–2016* 3. Han Kwang Sang *KPA Finance Department First Vice Director, 2010–2013* 4. Kim Chang Sop *Ministry of State Security Political Bureau Director, 2009–2015* 5. Kim Ki Nam *KWP Secretariat Agitation and Propaganda Secretary, 1992–2017* 6. Kim Kyong Hui *KWP Light Industry Department Director, 1987–2012* 7. Kim Kyong Ok *Organization & Guidance First Vice Director, 2008–2019* 8. Kim Phyong Hae *KWP Cadre Department Director, 2010–2016* 9. Kim Rak Hui *Cabinet Vice Premier 2010–2012* 10. Kim Yang Gon *KWP United Front Department, 2007–2015* 11. Jang Song Thaek *KWP Administration Department Director, 2007–2013* 12. Ju Kyu Chang *KWP Machine Industry Department Director, 2010–2016*	1. Choe Ik Gyu *KWP Agitation and Propaganda Department Director, March 2009 until September 2010 disappearance* 2. Hong Sok Hyong *KWP Planning & Finance Department Director, September 2010 until June 2011 disappearance* 3. Pak Nam Gi *KWP Planning & Finance Department Director, 2005 until March 2010 execution* 4. Pyon Yong Rip *Science & Technology General League Central Committee Chair from 2003 until 2010 removal* 5. Ri Je Gang *Organization & Guidance Department First Vice Director, 2001 until suspicious death in June 2010* 6. U Tong Chuk *Ministry of State Security First Vice Director, 2009 until late 2011 disappearance*

Table 2 (cont.)

Played important role in Kim Jong Un's inner circle (cont.)	Natural exit
13. Mun Kyong Dok KWP Pyongyang Chief Secretary, 2010–2014	1. Pak Jong Sun Organization & Guidance First Vice Director from 2010 until early 2011 death from lung cancer
14. O Kuk Ryol National Defense Commission Vice Chair, 2009–2014	
15. Pak To Chun KWP Secretariat Secretary, 2010–2015	2. Ri Chol Bong KWP Kangwon Provincial Committee Chief Secretary from 2006 until late 2009 car crash death
16. Ri Jae Il KWP Agitation and Propaganda Department First Vice Director, 2004–2020	
	Played less important role in Kim Jong Un's inner circle
17. Ri Ryong Ha KWP Administration Department First Vice Director, date unknown to 2013	1. Hong In Bom KWP South Pyongan Chief Secretary, 2010–2014
18. Thae Jong Su KWP General Services Department Director, September 2010 to May 2012	2. Ju Yong Sik KWP Chagang Chief Secretary, 2010–2012
	3. Ri Man Gon KWP North Pyongan Province Committee Chief Secretary, 2010–2015

Note: We omit Ju Sang Song and Ri Pyong Sam because we cannot confidently identify their positions.

Kim Jong Un's personality cult, notably Kim Ki Nam as KWP Secretariat Agitation and Propaganda Secretary. In terms of helping Kim govern and wield the power of the state, one task was notably absent among these elites; none of the elites that Kim Jong Il raised in prominence were involved in the Ministry of Public Security, essentially North Korea's police (Gause 2015: 266), although as KWP Administrative Department Director, Jang Song Thaek managed human resources in the security apparatus. Further, Kim Chang Sop was the Political

Bureau Director of the Ministry of State Security from 2009, which is North Korea's secret police and operates the concentration camps. Thus, between Kim Chang Sop, Kim Ki Nam, and Jang Song Thaek, Kim Jong Un had supportive allies who could provide control over the people. Overall, elites who were raised in prominence by Kim Jong Il played important roles in helping Kim Jong Un gain control over the 'infrastructural power' of the state (Mann 1984).

In contrast, as summarized in Table 3, only a few KWP elites who were not prominent in the post-stroke period were significant under Kim Jong Un pre-December 2013. Ri Thae Chol held the important position of First Vice Minister of the Ministry of Public Security, Kang Tong Yun held a significant role in the OGD, while several of these KWP elites moved to notable posts within the military. However, these were exceptions. The largest portion of KWP elites who were not raised up in prominence by Kim Jong Il played comparatively minor roles in Kim Jong Un's early years. Many held regional positions away from Pyongyang, others' primary roles were members of bodies that sound important but contain hundreds of members (the KWP Central Committee or the Supreme People's Assembly), while several held relatively insignificant roles (e.g., Choe Chil Nam as the Journalists' Union Central Committee Chair, Pak Kyong Son as North Korea-Laos Friend Association Chair, and Kim Yong Dae as the Korean Social Democratic Party Central Committee Chair).

As time passed though, Kim Jong Un even dispensed with KWP elites who Kim Jong Il had raised up in prominence for the former's power base. This included people like Choe Thae Bok (KWP education secretary) and Kim Kyong Hui (his aunt and the KWP light industry chief), neither of whom were purged, but both of whom became far less prominent post-succession. Thae Jong Su (KWP General Services), Ju Yong Sik (Chagang province chief secretary), and Han Kwang Sang (party finances) were all demoted in 2012 or 2013. While some very high-profile and important purges occurred post-succession, like that of Jang Song Thaek and his close associates, much of the power base was just gradually pushed out of the limelight and then eventually retired off or died in office.

How Kim Jong Un initially leaned on the KWP elites brought into a power base during his father's final years before dispensing with them as he consolidated power is reflected in the leadership event data. Figure 3 shows the probabilities of a KWP elite attending an event in Kim Jong Un's first two years, conditional on whether they were prominent in the period between Kim Jong Il's stroke (August 2008) and his death (December 17, 2011).[48] Figure 3 shows that, despite the

---

[48] The models that these probabilities are based on are in the Supplementary Materials, along with various robustness tests. The prominence of a KWP elite in this period is based on the proportion of events that they attended. In Figure 3, whether they are classified as prominent or not prominent reflects whether they were in the 1st or 99th percentile for this variable.

Table 3 Careers of KWP elites who were not raised in prominence by Kim Jong Il after his stroke, December 2011 to December 2013.

Played important role in Kim Jong Un's inner circle	Purged or retired under Kim Jong Il
1. Hwang Pyong So *Organization & Guidance Department Vice Director, 2005–2014*	1. Han Song Ryong *Removed from KWP Secretariat and Central Committee, September 2010*
2. Jon Pyong Ho *Cabinet Political Bureau Chief and Chief Secretary, September 2010 to March 2012*	2. Jong Ha Chol *Former KWP Agitation and Propaganda Department Chair, purged in 2005*
3. Kim Sung Yon *KWP Department Director, date unknown*	3. Kim Hyon Ju *Removed as Rason Party Chief Secretary, January 2010*
4. Kang Tong Yun *Organization and Guidance Department Vice Director, January 2007 to date unknown*	4. Kim Si Hak *Removed from Central Committee, September 2010*
5. Ri Ha Il *KPA Vice Marshal, date unknown*	5. Kim Tong Un *Removed as KWP Office 39 Director, February 2010*
6. Ri Thae Chol *Ministry of Public Security First Vice Director and Supreme Commander of Korean People's Internal Forces, May 2010 to date unknown*	6. Ri Kun Mo *Removed from Central Committee, September 2010*
7. Ri Yong Mu *National Defense Commission Vice Chair, 1998–2016*	7. Ri Tuk Nam *Removed as Kanggye City Party Secretary, December 2009*

Played less important role in Kim Jong Un's inner circle	Natural exit
1. Choe Chil Nam *Journalists' Union Central Committee Chair, October 2008 to April 2013*	1. Hong Song Nam *Died in March 2009*
2. Ho Jong Man *Chongryon Central Committee Chair, May 2010 to present*	2. Jang Song U *Died in August 2009*
	3. Jo Chang Dok *Died in 2013*
	4. Kim Ik Hyon *Died in January 2009*

Table 3 (cont.)

Played less important role in Kim Jong Un's inner circle (cont.)	Natural exit (cont.)
3. Jang Yong Sok *KWP Ryanggang Hyesan Chief Secretary, 2006–2019* 4. Ji Jae Ryong *Ambassador to China, September 2010–2021* 5. Ju Hak Sim *Samsu County Party Chief Secretary, 2006 to date unknown* 6. Kim Chol Man *Central Committee full member, September 2010–2018* 7. Kim Kyong Ho *Chair of Korea Taekwondo Committee, June 2011–2021* 8. Kim Kuk Thae *KWP Control Commission Head, 2010–2013* 9. Kim Pyong Sik *Phihyon County Party Committee Chief Secretary, date unknown* 10. Kim Un Gi *South Hwanghwe Party Chief Secretary, 1995 to date unknown* 11. Kim Yong Dae *Korean Social Democratic Party Central Committee Chair, 1998–2019* 12. Pak Kyong Son *North Korea-Laos Friend Association Chair, March 2010 to date unknown, and Ambassador to India, April 2013 to July 2014* 13. Pak Sun Hui *Supreme People's Assembly member, 2009–2014*	5. Kim Jung Rin *Died in April 2010* 6. Kim Yong Sam *Died in June 2009* 7. Pak Song Chol *Died in October 2008* 8. Ri Yong Chol *Died in April 2010* 9. Ryo Won *Died in July 2009* 10. So Man Sul *Died in February 2012*

Table 3 (cont.)

Played less important role in Kim Jong Un's inner circle (cont.)	Natural exit (cont.)
14. Rim Kyong Man *Rason Municipal Party Chief Secretary, January 2010–2011, and Party Central Committee Member, 2010 to present* 15. Ryu Mi Yong *Chondo Young Friends Party Central Committee Chair, 1993 –2016*	

Note: We omit Pak Jung Gun and Pak Min Gyun because we cannot identify confidently their positions.

earlier evidence that party elites were less likely over time to attend an event under Kim Jong Un, this was not initially the case for party elites who were prominent under Kim Jong Il after his stroke. In Kim Jong Un's first month, the probability of a party elite who had been prominent under Kim Jong Il after his stroke attending an event was about 0.95. This decreases marginally to just above 0.8 during Kim Jong Un's first year, but then rapidly decreases after that to about 0.45 by the time Kim Jong Un purges Jang Song Thaek. In sum, consistent with our theory, party elites who became increasingly prominent under Kim Jong Il when he was preparing for succession played key roles under Kim Jong Un after he initially took power, before he later marginalized them too.

4.5 Conclusion

In this section, we tested our arguments against the Kim Jong Il to Kim Jong Un transition in North Korea. Using novel data on thousands of leadership events in North Korea between 1994 and 2013, combined with original biographical data, we found evidence to support our arguments that (1) the outgoing dictator (Kim Jong Il) built up a power base of elites from outside their inner circle to help the successor (Kim Jong Un) govern and (2) although the successor reduced the size of his ruling coalition upon taking office, he initially refrained from marginalizing elites in his power base who could help him govern in his early years.

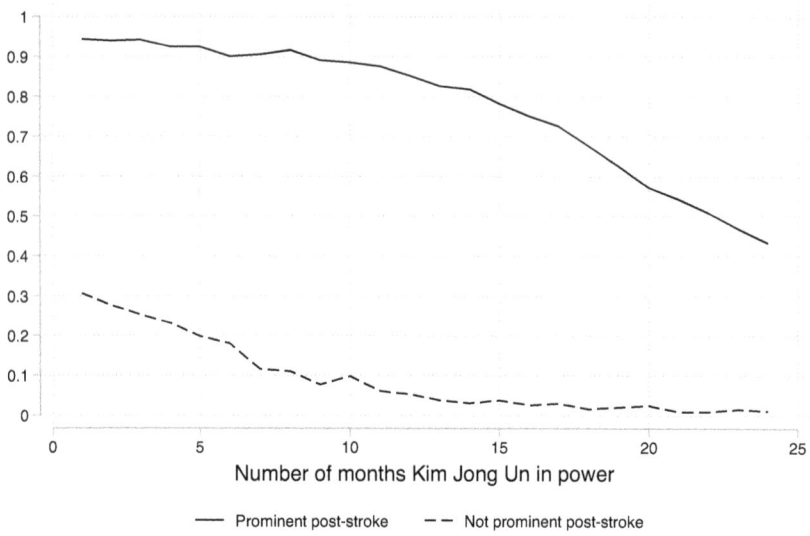

Figure 3 The probability of party elites attending an event, December 2011 to December 2013.

5 Comparative Applications

5.1 Introduction

The evidence from North Korea provides a comprehensive evidence base for the internal validity of how dictators manage elites to facilitate transition. But do these findings apply to other autocracies where personalist incumbents attempt to hand power to their chosen successor? We assess the external validity of our argument with qualitative case vignettes of elite management surrounding leadership transitions in party-based China, military Egypt, and monarchical Saudi Arabia. We select these cases to assess whether the arguments apply irrespective of ideology and institutional makeup, and whether the succession is hereditary.

5.2 Case Vignettes

5.2.1 China: Deng Xiaoping to Jiang Zemin

Few contemporary autocratic regimes have had as many successions as the Chinese Communist Party (CCP). The CCP's paramount leaders since 1949 run from Mao Zedong to Hua Guofeng, followed by Deng Xiaoping, Jiang Zemin, Hu Jintao, and Xi Jinping. Thus, there have been at least four regular leadership transitions under the CCP, five including Hua to Deng, which some scholars classify as irregular (Svolik 2012; cf. Chin et al. 2021). However, not all the transitions fall within our theory's scope; only Mao and Deng personalized power to a notable degree by the time they prepared for succession (Wright

2021). This point, combined with the brevity of Hua's time as China's paramount leader, led us to assess our theory against the Deng to Jiang transition.

Deng appointed Jiang as successor in June 1989, giving him the post of general secretary of the CCP. Despite Jiang taking on this role and shortly after also becoming chairman of the Central Military Commission in November 1989, Deng remained China's *de facto* leader. Jiang was previously Shanghai's mayor (1985–1987) and party secretary (1987–1989) before becoming the CCP's general secretary in the wake of the Tiananmen Square protests (Kuhn 2004: 164–74). Deng won the support of CCP elders for Jiang's candidacy, but Jiang was a relatively weak figure and had to contend with other ambitious powerful elites (Gilley 1998: 133, 138; Kuhn 2004: 163). President Yang Shangkun and his brother, General Yang Baibing, for instance, sought to solidify their position within Deng's camp and maneuver themselves favorably for a post-Deng world (Bachman 1996: 92; Joffe 1996: 312; Kuhn 2004: 213). Thus, establishing a power base within the top echelons of Chinese elite politics was critical for Jiang.

Jiang built a power base, with Deng's support, but this did not happen immediately. Despite officially retiring in November 1989, Deng remained China's paramount leader and acted as Jiang's protector while pushing for Jiang and the top leadership to move quicker with economic reforms (Gilley 1998: 177, 193; Kuhn 2004: 212–14). By the end of Deng's Southern Tour in 1992, during which Deng emphasized the "Reforms and Opening-Up" program in mainland China, Jiang had rallied behind Deng's reforms and gained Deng's confidence. Deng then anointed Jiang as the new paramount leader (Kuhn 2004: 214–16). Having acquired Deng's support, Jiang built a power base of elites from outside the top echelons of power. Jiang moved allies from Shanghai into key positions within the CCP central apparatus. Ding Guangen was moved to lead the CCP's propaganda department, Ba Zhongtan was put in charge of the country's paramilitary forces, and Jiang put his right-hand man, Zeng Qinghong, in charge of the CCP's General Office, which handles daily life and organizational matters at the top of the CCP (Gilley 1998, 198–9). Jiang's successor as Shanghai party secretary, Zhu Rongji, was also elevated to head China's central bank in 1993, before becoming the premier in 1998 (Kuhn 2004: 233). Jiang cultivated allies in the military, going on inspection tours to the country's seven military regions, meeting commanders, some of whom were subsequently promoted to positions in the central leadership. In 1992, Fu Quanyou (military region commander for Lanzhou) was appointed to take over the General Logistics Department of the People's Liberation Army (PLA), Zhu Dunfa (military region commander for Guangzhou) was appointed to the position of commandant at the National Defense University, and Zhang Wannian (commander of the Jinan Region) was promoted to the PLA Chief of

General Staff (Shambaugh 2016: chap. 4). Thanks to his predecessor's support, Jiang was able to build a power base as he transitioned from *de jure* leader as general secretary to become China's *de facto* leader too.

Per our theory, Jiang then governed by leaning especially on elites in his power base. One of the major tasks following the collapse of the Soviet Union was to ensure that the CCP retained power. Jiang was aided by two key allies from Shanghai, Zeng Qinghong and Wang Huning, who were central to rebuilding the party's organizational capacity over society (Shambaugh 2016). To further deepen economic reforms, Jiang relied on Zhu Rongji, whose work significantly boosted central government revenues (Gilley 1998: 208). Zhu also implemented major reforms to the country's state-owned enterprises, privatizing many smaller firms, reformed the country's financial system to make it more profitable, and fostered price stability which had contributed to unrest in the late 1980s (Naughton 2007: 100–7). Jiang also used his allies to modernize the PLA. A major component was a campaign against corruption and the military's involvement in the economy. From 1993 to 1999, with support from allies including Zhang Wannian, Jiang compelled the PLA to divest from military-run businesses (Mulvenon 2001: chaps. 6–7). In sum, elites whose prominence was heightened through becoming a member of Jiang's power base played key roles in helping Jiang accomplish the early major tasks facing his leadership.

Again, consistent with our theory, Jiang made some, albeit limited, progress in consolidating power by marginalizing Deng-era elites. Chen Xitong, the Beijing party secretary, was removed in 1995 after being implicated in a corruption scandal (Gilley 1998: 241–4). Jiang also purged the chair of the National People's Congress, Qiao Shi, in 1997, who was a major figure in the security apparatus (Gilley 1998: 306).[49] Party elders had pushed for Qiao Shi to be given the state presidency to lessen Jiang's power, but Jiang managed to retain his positions. The elders were reprimanded but did not face serious sanction, and Qiao Shi was similarly "only" retired. Chinese politics was characterized by 'elite liberalization' in this era, where elites rarely faced serious sanctions for agitating for a preferred policy or candidate, even if they lost their formal standing (Dittmer 2003: 105–6).

However, Jiang did not later notably marginalize elites from his own power base to further consolidate power. This is related to the limited progress Jiang made in marginalizing Deng-era elites. Jiang had to rule in coalition with other groups (Teiwes 2000: 76–80). Some party elders held significant sway, as did other factions. Jiang therefore had to keep members of his (primarily Shanghai originated) power base close because he would have otherwise depended on

---

[49] The NPC vice chair, Tian Jiyun, was also removed in 1998 (Dittmer 2003: 115).

prominent elites who did not owe their career to him. These individuals had achieved their standing thanks to promotions from the previous generation of leaders, meaning their base of support preceded Jiang's rise (Kou and Zang 2013: 11). However, other successors, including Kim Jong Il and Kim Jong Un in North Korea, have successfully marginalized their predecessor's key supporters; so, why did Jiang comparatively struggle? It may be that Deng's continued presence, even behind the scenes, restricted Jiang's actions (Leber et al. 2023). The extent of Deng's influence was apparent through his choice of Hu Jintao as Jiang's successor, over Jiang's preference for Zeng Qinghong (Lam 2006: 21; Shambaugh 2016). Thus, although the case largely conforms to our theory, it highlights the possible scope condition of successors being able to marginalize their predecessor's allies only if the predecessor left office through a natural death.

5.2.2 Egypt: Anwar Sadat to Hosni Mubarak

We now assess our theory against the transition in Egypt from Anwar Sadat to Hosni Mubarak in 1981. Strictly speaking, the case lies outside the scope of our theory since Sadat was assassinated rather than exiting office regularly. However, in all other aspects the case falls within our theory.[50] Sadat established a personalist autocracy, he prepared for succession to his preferred choice (Mubarak), and the autocratic regime did not change when Mubarak came to power. We therefore expect to observe the management of elites described by our theory between 1975 and 1981, once Sadat chose Mubarak as his successor, and in the years following Sadat's death.

Prior to the transition to Mubarak, Sadat consolidated power by purging many of the other senior participants of the 1952 Free Officers' revolution that had brought his predecessor, Gamal Abdel Nasser, to power. Those who disagreed with his policies were quietly retired or pushed to the periphery, and active-duty officers who retained positions in the core elite were restricted to the roles of staff subordinates with a limited authority of office (Hinnesbusch 1983: 30; Kandil 2016: 284–8). Thus, using many of the same tactics of elite management that Kim Jong Il employed to consolidate power after coming to office – emasculating and purging elites (see Section 3) – Sadat successfully personalized his leadership.[51]

---

[50] There are also few cases of succession in personalist military dictatorships because in the time it takes for dictators to personalize power, military leaders often either fall from office or transition their regime to a party-based regime, having "won" an election, to give themselves more proclaimed legitimacy to govern (Geddes et al. 2014).

[51] The Nasser to Sadat transition falls outside the scope of our theory since, despite being Nasser's vice president at the time of Nasser's death, Sadat was not Nasser's choice of successor (Beattie 2000: 34; Cook 2012: 117).

As Sadat's preferred successor, Mubarak was put in a position to build a power base.[52] As vice president, Mubarak was entrusted by Sadat to supervise the presidential administration and the cabinet, as well as conduct important diplomatic missions. This allowed Mubarak to build a profile among the country's elites but also insert allies into important ministries like the Ministry of Foreign Affairs. Correspondingly, many of the individuals who Mubarak brought into his power base at this time were diplomats and military officers (Springborg 2018: 30–1). For example, in Section 2, we identified Abu Ghazala as one of these key individuals. Ghazala was Egypt's military attaché to Washington between 1976 and 1979; he helped develop the relationship with the United States, became the chief of general staff in 1979, and the minister of defense from 1981 to 1989 (Springborg 1987: 6). Sadat also gave Mubarak control over the ruling National Democratic Party (NDP) and the country's armed forces, while Sadat continued to retire powerful elites from his generation who had established Egypt's military autocracy (Waterbury 1983: xiv–xv). Ultimately, consistent with our theory, Sadat helped Mubarak establish and solidify his position as a powerful figure in Egyptian politics, moving beyond his traditional fiefdom of the air force. This strengthened Mubarak's position. When Sadat was assassinated in 1981, there were no major alternative centers of power and Mubarak was unchallenged within the regime for the presidency (Cook 2012: 157–8).

When Mubarak became president, our theory expects that he should move against high-ranking members of Sadat's inner circle to consolidate power for himself. Accordingly, Mubarak purged the country's ruling party and civilian elite of Sadat loyalists. He kept most of the cabinet in place for the first four years but immediately began expelling members from the ruling NDP, firing ministers who were allegedly involved in corruption and bringing in new cadres to the NDP (Arafat 2009: 24–6). He also purged major business clients of Sadat and begun to cultivate new networks of business elites that would support his regime (El Tarouty 2015: 47–9). Overall, Mubarak replaced more than half the NDP politburo, two-thirds of the secretariat, 60 percent of its standing committee, and the speaker of the legislature (Springborg 2018: 158).

Consistent with our theory, Mubarak did not purge everyone upon entering office. He appointed key allies to the secretary general of the

---

[52] Sadat handpicked Mubarak to become vice president in April 1975, he sometimes issued presidential decrees transferring his powers to Mubarak for limited periods (e.g., when he went on holiday), and he said that the leadership should be handed over to the 'October generation,' which referred to those (including Mubarak) who led the Yom Kippur War against Israel (Eilts 1978; El Tohamy 1981).

NDP (General Yusuf Wali), the assistant secretary position (General Kamal Shazli), as well as empowering the military, which, as discussed, was crucial to his power base (Springborg 2018: 158). Mubarak massively increased military spending, which had fallen significantly during Sadat's later years (Kennedy 2017: 110). Initially, Mubarak's key ally, the Minister of Defense Abu Ghazala, was allowed to amass significant economic and political influence, and Mubarak also appointed several military figures to the cabinet (Kennedy 2017: 113). However, Mubarak increasingly viewed Ghazala as a rival and purged him in 1989 following accusations that he was involved in smuggling weapons to Iraq and North Korea (Kandil 2016: 305–6). Ultimately, the fall of Abu Ghazala, previously believed to be a potential successor to Mubarak (Central Intelligence Agency 1987: 3–5), marked the consolidation of Mubarak's rule.

5.2.3 Saudi Arabia: King Salman to Mohammed bin Salman

Finally, we assess our theory against a case of monarchical succession in Saudi Arabia from King Salman to Mohammed bin Salman (MbS). At the time of writing (August 2024), the 88-year-old King Salman remains Saudi's *de jure* leader. Some scholars argue that the transition has essentially already happened, and that MbS is Saudi's "effective ruler" (Stenslie 2018: 61). However, although Saudi's high-profile policies bear MbS's fingerprints – the blockade of Qatar, the war in Yemen, women being allowed to drive, Vision 2030 (Habibi 2019; Stenslie 2018: 62) – his authority rests on his father's support (Gause 2018: 75; Herb 2022: 117).[53] We can therefore only assess the pre-transition aspects of elite management predicted by our theory. The transition's global importance though, given Saudi's economic and geostrategic significance, provides value to assessing how well our theory explains preparations for succession in Saudi thus far, while its incomplete nature permits brief predictions about future elite management.

We expect to observe the construction of a power base of elites from outside King Salman's inner circle from the time that Salman appointed MbS as crown prince, and thereby the designated successor, in June 2017. King Salman ascended to the throne in January 2015 following the death of his half-brother, King Abdullah. King Salman originally appointed another half-brother, Muqrin bin Abdulaziz, as crown prince; this would have kept the succession within the

---

[53] There were rumors of a rift between King Salman and MbS following the murder of Saudi dissident journalist, Jamal Khashoggi, and reported disagreements over policies including the war in Yemen (Kirchgaessner and Hopkins 2019; see also Willner 2022: 372), although Stenslie (2020: 357) emphasizes that these rumors should not be weighted too heavily given the extensive political capital that King Salman has invested in MbS.

second generation.[54] However, after only a few months in April 2015, King Salman named his nephew, Muhammed bin Nayef (MbN), as the new crown prince (Gause 2018: 80). This was a seismic moment since MbN was not from the second generation, but MbN was otherwise a logical choice given his experience in government, including maintaining internal security against threats from radical Islamic terrorism, and he was respected in Washington, DC, a significant consideration due to the importance of the US partnership for Saudi security (Gause 2018: 81; Stenslie 2018: 67–8). But King Salman dismissed MbN in June 2017, replacing him with his son, MbS (Stenslie 2018: 69).[55] King Salman may have been preparing for succession to MbS prior to this, having named MbS as defense minister in January 2015 (Stenslie 2016: 125). June 2017, however, marks the official moment that MbS became King Salman's designated successor. From this point, if our theory is accurate, we should observe the construction of a power base to help MbS govern when he becomes king.

Upon becoming crown prince, MbS needed to and has constructed a power base. In his first year as crown prince, MbS's youth and inexperience meant he had few allies within the ruling family, except for his father and younger brothers (Stenslie 2018: 70). Salman gave him leeway to change this. During his tenure as defense minister from January 2015, MbS oversaw a Saudi-led military intervention against the Houthi rebels in Yemen in April 2015, which Salman hoped would earn him respect among older and more senior royals. Salman helped him build support among the religious establishment by instructing the head of the royal court to refer all requests for grants from the religious establishment to MbS. Salman also appointed MbS to head a cabinet committee overseeing economic and social policy (Gause 2018; Stenslie 2016: 125–6). Regarding elite management, MbS raised up in prominence younger princes, nonroyal advisors, and even some foreigners to construct a power base. MbS appointed members of the royal family's fourth generation who are below him in the hierarchy but close to him in age to subcabinet positions in Riyadh and positions of authority in the regional governates (Gause 2018: 83); Fahd bin Mohammed al-Essa, who had been the head of MbS's office at the Defense Ministry, was brought in to head the royal court (Stenslie 2020: 360–1); and MbS even brought in Hosni Mubarak's former security chief, Habib al-Adly, to

---

[54] The House of Saud's founding monarch was King Abdulaziz bin Abdul Rahman Al Saud. He passed on power to his second son, Saud bin Abdulaziz Al Saud. Power has then passed between Al Saud's sons, sometimes violently and sometimes peacefully. The prospective transition from King Salman to MbS would therefore be Saudi's first intergenerational transfer of power since 1953 (Stenslie 2018: 70).

[55] On MbS's surprising rise, given his lack of experience, and his mother's role in positioning him as King Salman's successor, see Stenslie (2016: 124).

advise him on his purported anti-corruption campaign (Stenslie 2018: 70). In sum, as our theory predicts, King Salman has prepared for succession by empowering MbS to construct a power base of relatively outsider elites.

Our theory also expects though that incumbents should not purge incumbent-era elites if they are visibly weakened when preparing for succession. Salman's old age, visible frailty following a stroke before becoming king, and rumored dementia suggest he should not have risked purging prominent elites to facilitate succession to MbS (Stenslie 2018: 62). And yet, to a certain extent he has permitted this. The infamous purges from 2017 that MbS orchestrated – where hundreds of prominent officials were detained at the Ritz-Carlton Hotel under accusations of anti-corruption – included the removal of Mitab bin Abdullah, who was commander of the 100,000-strong National Guard. Prince Walid bin Talal, the then richest man in the Middle East, and Khalid Al Tuwaijiri, the former chief of the royal court and the highest ranking nonroyal under King Salman's predecessor, King Abdullah, were also caught up in the purges (Gause 2018: 82; Stenslie 2018: 61).

However, the arrests of high-ranking princes were the exception rather than the norm. Most targets, even if some were extended members of the ruling family, were business elites.[56] Additionally, observers of Saudi politics predict that these purges should have the effects described in the logic of our theory. We expect that visibly weak incumbents should not purge prominent elites when preparing for succession because it could be destabilizing. Scholars of Saudi politics agree, writing that these purges provoked anger and may precipitate a challenge to King Salman or to MbS when King Salman dies (Gause 2018: 82–3; Stenslie 2018: 69).

Assuming MbS takes power regularly, through King Salman's natural death or abdication, how is MbS likely to manage Saudi elites? Since our theory predicts a marginalization of incumbent-era elites, we expect that he will further marginalize prominent royals from the second and third generations (Gause 2018: 82). He should govern initially by leaning on elites in the power base constructed since June 2017, notably fourth-generation royals. However, our theory expects that after an initial period, MbS should then look to marginalize these elites to prevent them becoming too powerful. Since many fourth-generation royals are a similar age to MbS, they *could* get restless at MbS's monopolization of power (Kokkonen and Sundell 2014: 440). MbS's drive to diversify Saudi's economy could provide an opportune moment to

---

[56] The purges were likely intended to shock Saudi's business community into behaving more cleanly and drive greater investment moving forward, or simply boost MbS's coffers (Gause 2018: 76–8).

bring in fifth-generation royals – under the pretext that they have expertise beyond oil – once they become of age (Habibi 2019).

5.3 Conclusion

The evidence of how personalist autocrats and their successors manage elites to facilitate succession in these party-based, military, and monarchical regimes largely supports our argument. There are some discrepancies. King Salman and MbS have treated existing elites more aggressively than our theory suggests they should, although this may be a misstep on their part. It may also be harder for successors to marginalize elites to consolidate power when the predecessor is still alive (per the case of Jiang Zemin). Beyond these points though, the case vignettes are consistent with our theory, suggesting it explains how dictators manage elites to facilitate succession in autocracies with personalistic incumbents from across the world.

6 Conclusion: Implications, Future Succession, and Further Research

Mancur Olson (1993: 572) wrote that "most dictatorships are by their nature especially susceptible to succession crises." Yet, as we highlighted in Section 1, many have carried out leadership transitions in recent years. How are they doing it? Recent comparative empirical research shows that autocrats can use institutional strategies to alleviate uncertainty surrounding succession, but this is only part of the story (Kokkonen and Sundell 2014; Kokkonen et al. 2022; Meng 2020, 2021).

In this Element, we have highlighted the importance of the noninstitutional tool of elite management to facilitating succession in autocracies with personalistic incumbents. We presented evidence from North Korea to support this argument. North Korea is rarely used to test comparative theories about autocracy but in this case North Korean leadership transitions were helpful since they permitted clear identification of when autocrats were preparing for succession and attempting to consolidate the transition. Evidence from North Korea and comparative vignettes was largely consistent with the theory: Dictators and their successors facilitate succession by constructing a power base for the successor from elites outside of the incumbent's inner circle. Then, once in office, successors initially rely on this power base to govern, but they marginalize ruling elites from their predecessor's era before also targeting officials in their power base to further consolidate power. We close by discussing several academic and policy implications, consider what the findings suggest about possible future succession in North Korea, and highlight three promising areas for further research.

6.1 Implications

Autocrats manage elites in a distinct manner when they prepare for succession. More broadly then, do an autocrat's actions vary based on the leader's time horizon? This points to important questions for further research, which we return to in Section 6.3, but it also suggests that analyzing autocratic elite management can yield insights about the likelihood of future policy shifts and even the probability of leadership turnover occurring as well as forecasting the identity of the successor.

The evidence also highlights the importance of understanding the mechanisms behind observable behaviors in dictatorships to avoid making mistaken inferences about how these opaque regimes operate. Timoneda (2020) and Woldense (2022) provide compelling evidence that dictators increase the size of their ruling coalition at times of vulnerability as a coup-proofing measure. However, this Element shows that this is not the only reason why dictators might increase the size of their ruling coalition. Autocrats may also enlarge their ruling coalition to build a power base for the successor. The multiple mechanisms that drive this possible outcome illustrate the importance of gathering insights from insider sources, where possible, to better understand what strategies drive behavior within autocracies.

Finally, the Element shows how systematic analysis of leadership event data can be instructive for practitioners. The prominence or marginalization of officials is sometimes evident at leadership events before institutional changes are publicly known. In North Korea, one recent example of this is the military elite, Pak Jong Chon, who received a big promotion to vice marshal in May 2020. Pak was known to analysts of North Korea before May 2020, but his importance was not fully realized. However, his rising status was visible prior to May 2020 in the leadership event data as he was the most prominent elite in North Korea between January 1, 2020, and April 12, 2020 (Kim Jong Un's last event prior to his disappearance that year; see Section 6.2).[57] Elsewhere, Qin Gang's removal as China's foreign minister in July 2023 was precipitated by his disappearance for a few weeks from public events (McDonell et al. 2023). These kinds of insights have practical applications. For example, the prominence of elites at public events, including diplomats, may correspond to them having the favor, trust, and authority of the leader when conducting negotiations. Hence, diplomats consistently prominent at leadership events should be

---

[57] Pak attended eight out of seventeen events in this period; no other elite attended more than five.

the most fruitful counterparts in negotiations. Analysts should of course monitor other sources, including formal membership of institutions, to glean insights into elites' roles and status. But our work shows the value for policymakers, including those involved in Track One and Track Two diplomacy with North Korea, of systematically analyzing leadership event data.

6.2 Future Succession

The rise of Kim Jong Un and his consolidation of power surprised many observers. However, rumors have swirled since the Covid-19 pandemic about Kim's health and the long-term viability of his rule. His extended disappearance from public in 2020 prompted speculation about his health. Analysts speculated that internal party changes in 2021, including the creation of a deputy party leadership position (a new First Secretary position), are mechanisms for emergency succession; these added to the perception that Kim Jong Un's leadership was more fragile than it had hitherto appeared (Lankov 2021; Zwirko 2021). Concurrently, the growing prominence of Kim Jong Un's younger sister, Kim Yo Jong, led some to suggest she might be the *de facto* deputy or that she may become the interim leader if Kim Jong Un suffers an untimely and sudden demise (Cha and Katz 2023).

Perhaps most dramatic, however, has been the sudden emergence of Kim Jong Un's daughter, Kim Ju Ae, at public events alongside her father from late 2022 (O'Carroll and Reddy 2022). It is not yet clear what role Kim Ju Ae will play, but her appearances raise questions about the regime's leadership planning. Indeed, there are signs that she is being groomed for a leadership role, with the North Korean press describing her as one of two "great persons of guidance" alongside her father, using terminology generally only associated with her father, grandfather, and great-grandfather (Cheong 2024; Rodong Sinmun 2024). Yet she is believed to have been born in 2013, and so will not legally become an adult until around 2031. Even then, she would almost certainly need further education before she could be anointed successor. However, her grandfather's and father's ascents to power indicate that it might not be that long before she could theoretically be anointed as successor.

Kim Jong Il was thirty-two when he was secretly appointed successor and thirty-nine when he was publicly unveiled. He then had fourteen years supporting his father's leadership before Kim Il Sung died in 1994 (Cheong 2011: chap. 2). Kim Jong Il received training and gained experience in politics and administrative decision-making while in university, and then his father helped him build a power base in the central party apparatus. He also had valuable childhood experiences in the country, being schooled alongside other members of the top elite, helping to build valuable friendships from a young age (see Section 3). By contrast, Kim Jong Un was partially educated overseas and was not well integrated into elite social networks as a child. He was hurriedly designated successor at twenty-four, unveiled at twenty-six, and began running the country at twenty-seven.

Neither Kim Ju Ae's father nor her grandfather made public appearances prior to being publicly announced as successor. Hence, her appearance, if she is to become the successor, places her in uncharted territory. Kim Il Sung was not afraid to appoint direct blood relatives like his brother (Kim Yong Ju) and his uncle (Kang Ryang Uk) to positions of power. Similarly, Kim Jong Il gave his sister (Kim Kyong Hui) a prominent position in the central party, as has Kim Jong Un (Kim Yo Jong). Thus, it may be that Kim Ju Ae will become another family member handed positions and responsibilities within the regime, rather than being the future leader. Another important factor to consider is the prominent role that Kim Jong Un has thus far accorded his wife Ri Sol Ju (Tertitskiy 2018). Kim Jong Un appears to be interested in cultivating the image of a loving husband and father. The emergence of his daughter may therefore also be part of such image building, but it appears that this is not his sole intention.

Coverage of her appearances in the North Korean press is instructive on this point. Analysis of photographs and accompanying descriptions of her appearances in the press indicate that Kim Ju Ae is being vested with a higher status than her aunt, for instance, who is a high-level party official (Cheong 2023; Tertitskiy 2023). The decision to present her meeting with senior military officers and show them deferentially bowing to her also appears to signal special status, unmatched by other family members who have held important positions.

Despite these signs, however, it remains to be seen whether Kim Jong Un is planning a succession, and whether his daughter will become his preferred candidate. If the last two successions are a guide, the identity of the successor was not set in stone until a candidate has been designated internally. However, if Kim Ju Ae is being groomed to take the reins, and what has come before is a guide, there are several patterns of elite management that our research suggests we might observe. First, Kim Ju Ae would need a power base of loyal officials to help her wield the power of the state as she embarks on succeeding her father. This would likely include officials working in the party's human resources department (the OGD), communications specialists (the APD), the security services, and munitions experts (the Military Industry Department). Today, the OGD is headed by one of her father's most trusted lieutenants, Jo Yong Won, while her aunt is deputy director of the APD. Second, Kim Ju Ae's associations with the people charged with overseeing these departments will likely deepen in the coming decade(s), and she may receive practical experience working in these departments, perhaps under the stewardship of her aunt or other close confidants of her father. Third, succession would likely not lead to a significant loss of power for the military. Just as Kim Jong Il refrained from marginalizing military officials when preparing for succession (see Section 4), Kim Jong Un would also likely be similarly wary of attempting to sideline military elites given their currently prominent status in the regime as well as Kim's possible health issues.

A fourth generation of a ruling family would be almost unprecedented for modern dictatorships. However, North Korea's Kim regime has well-established practices of elite management that could allow Kim Ju Ae to become North Korea's next and first female leader.

6.3 Further Research

This Element's findings point to several fruitful areas for further research. First, future work should examine whether the elite management strategies that we identify are effective at facilitating succession. While recent prior research on autocratic leadership succession has examined the effectiveness of institutionalized rules on the likelihood of succession occurring (Kokkonen and Sundell 2014; Kokkonen et al. 2022; Meng 2020, 2021), our goal was more circumspect. We simply sought to identify how incumbents manage elites to prepare for succession, and how successors manage elites to secure the transition once they come to office. Evidence from North Korea suggests that these tactics are effective, or at least not ineffective, but such claims are currently speculative and should be tested. Collecting additional elite-level data across dictatorships can facilitate testing of these relationships alongside alternative explanations of how autocratic regimes pull off succession.

More generally, scholars have only scratched the surface of succession in autocracies. A second important question is to examine how less personalistic autocrats prepare for succession. Our argument applies exclusively to personalistic incumbents because it relies on autocrats being able to manipulate the status of elites. But non-personalist autocrats also often try to influence the identity of their successor. In heavily institutionalized Vietnam, for instance, the less personalistic Nong Duc Manh helped position Nguyen Phu Trong as his successor (Koh 2012: 366). Understanding the noninstitutional strategies that such dictators employ can lead to a fuller picture of the strategies that autocrats employ to prepare for succession.

Finally, future work should examine policy effects related to succession. For instance, how is policy affected by impending succession as autocrats near the end of their expected tenure, either due to their age or because they are adhering to formalized rules that imply that they should leave office? Do autocrats become more or less risk-averse? Are there types of policies or goals that they are more likely to pursue before leaving office? Related work examines how external actors' views of an autocrat's position affect their policies toward autocracies (e.g., Bak 2016), but autocrats are also influential actors so understanding how their time horizon affects their policy decisions is worth studying. As Pepinsky (2014: 650) writes, "authoritarian regimes do many things besides grow/stagnate and survive/collapse." Studying succession's effects on policy can improve our understanding of how these regular events affect the lives of the billions of people who live under autocracy.

References

Aaskoven, L., & Nyrup, J. (2021). Performance and Promotions in an Autocracy: Evidence from Nazi Germany. *Comparative Politics*, 54(1), 51–74.

Arafat, A. (2009). *Hosni Mubarak and the Future of Democracy in Egypt*, Palgrave.

Bachman, D. (1996). Succession, Consolidation, and Transition in China's Future. *Journal of Northeast Asian Studies*, 15(1), 89–106.

Bak, D. (2016). Political Investment Cycles in Democracies and Autocracies. *International Interactions*, 42(5), 797–819.

Beardsworth, N., Cheeseman, N., & Tinhu, S. (2019). Zimbabwe: The Coup That Never Was, and the Election That Could Have Been. *African Affairs*, 118(472), 580–96.

Beattie, K. (2000). *Egypt during the Sadat Years*, Palgrave.

Bennett, B., & Lind, J. (2011). The Collapse of North Korea: Military Missions and Requirements. *International Security*, 36(2), 84–119.

Brownlee, J. (2007). Hereditary Succession in Modern Autocracies. *World Politics*, 59(4), 595–628.

Bueno de Mesquita, B., & Smith, A. (2017). Political Succession: A Model of Coups, Revolution, Purges, and Everyday Politics. *Journal of Conflict Resolution*, 61(4), 707–43.

Bueno de Mesquita, B., Smith, A., Siverson, R., & Morrow, J. (2003). *The Logic of Political Survival*, MIT Press.

Buzo, A. (2018). *Politics and Leadership in North Korea: The Guerilla Dynasty*, Routledge.

Byman, D., & Lind, J. (2010). Pyongyang's Survival Strategy: Tools of Authoritarian Control in North Korea. *International Security*, 35(1), 44–74.

Central Intelligence Agency. (1987). Egypt after Mubarak: The Succession Question. *Directorate of Intelligence*, February 1987. www.cia.gov/readingroom/docs/CIA-RDP06T00412R000606630001-9.pdf.

CGTN. (2023). Côte d'Ivoire VP Daniel Duncan Resigns Due to Personal Reasons: Presidency. *CGTN*, June 16. https://africa.cgtn.com/cote-divoire-vp-daniel-duncan-resigns-due-to-personal-reasons-presidency/.

Cha, V. (2011). China's Newest Province? *New York Times*, December 20. www.nytimes.com/2011/12/20/opinion/will-north-korea-become-chinas-newest-province.html.

References

Cha, V. & Katz, K. (2023). Unanswered Questions about North Korean Leadership. *Center for Strategic & International Studies*, March 14. www.csis.org/analysis/unanswered-questions-about-north-korean-leadership-0.

Cheong, S. (2010). The Formalization of a System for Achieving Kim Jong-Un's Succession to North Korean Leadership and the Changing Power Structure in the North [김정은 후계체계의 공식화와 북한 권력체계 변화]. *North Korean Studies Research* [북한견구학회보], 14(2), 159–88.

Cheong, S. (2011). *The Contemporary North Korean Politics: History, Ideology, and Power System* [현대북한의 정치: 역사, 신념, 권력체계], Sejong Institute.

Cheong, S. (2023). Eight Reasons Why Kim Ju Ae Can Be Considered the Internally Designated Succession to Kim Jong Un. *Sejong Institute.* https://sejong.org/web/boad/22/egoread.php?bd=22&itm=&txt=&pg=1&seq=6967.

Cheong, S. (2024). Assessing the Meaning of the Expression "Great Person of Guidance" in Reference to Kim Ju Ae [김주애에 대한 '향도의 위대한 분' 표현 사용 의미 평가], *Irounnet*, March 25. www.eroun.net/news/articleView.html?idxno=41355.

Chin, J., Carter, D., & Wright, J. (2021). The Varieties of Coups D'état: Introducing the Colpus Dataset. *International Studies Quarterly*, 65(4), 1040–51.

Chin, J., Escribà-Folch, A., Song, W., & Wright, J. (2022). Reshaping the Threat Environment: Personalism, Coups, and Assassinations. *Comparative Political Studies*, 55(4), 657–87.

Chin, J., Song, W., & Wright, J. (2023). Personalization of Power and Mass Uprisings in Dictatorships. *British Journal of Political Science*, 53(1), 25–44.

Choe, H. (2023). [Pyongyang NOW] On the First Anniversary of His Death, Held Up as "Long-time Loyal Servant of the Third Succession" Who Is Hyon Chol Hae [사망 1주기에 띄우는 '3대세습 만고충신' 현철해는 누구]. *Yonhap*, May 22. www.yna.co.kr/view/AKR20230522108700535.

Collier, D. (2011). Understanding Process Tracing. *PS: Political Science & Politics*, 44(4), 823–30.

Cook, S. (2012). *The Struggle for Egypt: From Nasser to Tahrir Square*, Oxford University Press.

Cumings, B. (2012). The Kim's Three Bodies: Communism and Dynastic Succession in North Korea. *Current History*, 111(746), 216–22.

Dahl, R. (1971). *Polyarchy: Participation and Opposition*, Yale University Press.

De Bruin, E. (2020). *How to Prevent Coups d'État: Counterbalancing and Regime Survival*, Cornell University Press.

Decalo, S. (1989). *Psychoses of Power: African Personal Dictatorships*, Routledge.

Dittmer, L. (2003). Chinese Factional Politics under Jiang Zemin. *Journal of East Asian Studies*, 3(1), 97–128.

Dukalskis, A. (2017). *The Authoritarian Public Sphere: Legitimation and Autocratic Power in North Korea, Burma, and China*, Routledge.

Dukalskis, A. (2021). *Making the World Safe for Dictatorship*, Oxford University Press.

Eberstadt, N., Rubin, M., & Tretyakova, A. (1995). The Collapse of Soviet and Russian Trade with the DPRK, 1989–1993: Impact and Implications. *International Journal of Korean Unification Studies*, 4, 87–104.

Eilts, H. (1978). Hermann Eilts (US Ambassador to Egypt) to Cyrus Vance. *US Department of State*, October 12. https://aad.archives.gov/aad/createpdf?rid=251008&dt=2694&dl=2009.

El Tarouty, S. (2015). *Businessmen, Clientelism, and Authoritarianism in Egypt*, Palgrave.

El Tohamy, O. (1981). Egypt's Hosni Mubarak Picks Up Sadat's Reins: Profile. *The Christian Science Monitor*, October 14. www.csmonitor.com/1981/1014/101447.html/%28page%29/2.

Escribà-Folch, A. (2012). Authoritarian Responses to Foreign Pressure: Spending, Repression, and Sanctions. *Comparative Political Studies*, 45(6), 683–713.

Fails, M. (2020). Oil Income and the Personalization of Autocratic Politics. *Political Science Research and Methods*, 8(4), 772–9.

Fifield, A. (2019). *The Great Successor: The Divinely Perfect Destiny of Brilliant Comrade Kim Jong Un*, Hachette UK.

Finer. S. (1962). *The Man on Horseback: The Role of the Military in Politics*, Pall Mall Press.

Frantz, E., & Stein, E. (2017). Countering Coups: Leadership Succession Rules in Dictatorships. *Comparative Political Studies*, 50(7), 935–62.

Fujimoto, K. (2003). *Kim Jong Il's Chef*, Wolgan Chosun.

Gandhi, J. (2008). *Political Institutions under Dictatorship*, Cambridge University Press.

Gandhi, J., & Sumner, J. (2020). Measuring the Consolidation of Power in Nondemocracies. *Journal of Politics*, 82(4), 1545–58.

Gause, F. (2018). Fresh Prince: The Schemes and Dreams of Saudi Arabia's Next King. *Foreign Affairs*, 97(3), 75–86.

Gause, K. (2011). *North Korea under Kim Chong-il: Power, Politics, and Prospects for Change*, ABC-CLIO.

Gause, K. (2015). *North Korean House of Cards: Leadership Dynamics under Kim Jong-un*, Committee for Human Rights in North Korea.

Geddes, B., Wright, J., & Frantz, E. (2014). Autocratic Breakdown and Regime Transitions: A New Data Set. *Perspectives on Politics*, 12(3), 313–31.

Geddes, B., Wright, J., & Frantz, E. (2018). *How Dictatorships Work: Power, Personalization, and Collapse*, Cambridge University Press.

Gerschewski, J. (2013). The Three Pillars of Stability: Legitimation, Repression, and Co-optation in Autocratic Regimes. *Democratization*, 20(1), 13–38.

Gerschewski, J. (2023). *The Two Logics of Autocratic Rule*, Cambridge University Press.

Gilley, B. (1998). *Tiger on the Brink: Jiang Zemin and China's New Elite*, University of California Press.

Goemans, H. (2008). Which Way Out? The Manner and Consequences of Losing Office. *Journal of Conflict Resolution*, 52(6), 771–94.

Goemans, H., Gleditsch, K., & Chiozza, G. (2009). Introducing Archigos: A Dataset of Political Leaders. *Journal of Peace Research*, 46(2), 269–83.

Goldring, E., & Matthews, A. (2023). To Purge or Not to Purge? An Individual-Level Quantitative Analysis of Elite Purges in Dictatorships. *British Journal of Political Science*, 53(2), 575–93.

Goldring, E., & Matthews, A. (2024). Brothers in Arms No Longer: Who Do Regime Change Coup-Entry Dictators Purge? *Journal of Conflict Resolution*, 68(10), 1913–40.

Goldring, E., & Ward, P. (2024). Elite Management before Autocratic Leader Succession: Evidence from North Korea. *World Politics*, 76(3), 417–56.

Ha, J. (2014). North Korean Escapee Kim Cheol-jin's Chronicles of Pyongyang ② The Inside Story of the Frunze Academy Incident, The North Korean Version of Valkyrie That Ended in Failure [탈북자 김철진의 평양실록 ② 프룬제 군사아카데미야 사건의 내막 실패로 끝난 북한판 '발키리' 프룬제 사건]. *Wolgan Chosun*, 9.

Habibi, N. (2019). Implementing Saudi Arabia's Vision 2030: An Interim Balance Sheet. *Middle East Brief*, 127, 1–9.

Haggard, S., & Noland, M. (2007). *Famine in North Korea: Markets, Aid, and Reform*, Columbia University Press.

Haggard, S., Herman, L., & Ryu, J. (2014). Political Change in North Korea: Mapping the Succession. *Asian Survey*, 54(4), 773–800.

Han, K. (2009). The Organizational Behavior and Bureaucratic Politics in North Korea's Decision-Making Process: Expansion and Retreat of Economic Reform, 2000~2009 [북한 정책결정과정의 조직행태와 관료정치: 경제

개혁 확대 및 후퇴를 중심으로(2000~09)], PhD Dissertation, Kyungnam University.

Hassan, M. (2020). *Regime Threats and State Solutions: Bureaucratic Loyalty and Embeddedness in Kenya*, Cambridge University Press.

Hassan, M., Mattingly, D., & Nugent, E. (2022). Political Control. *Annual Review of Political Science*, 25, 155–74.

Helms, L. (2020). Leadership Succession in Politics: The Democracy/Autocracy Divide Revisited. *The British Journal of Politics and International Relations*, 22(2), 328–46.

Herb, M. (2022). The Decay of Family Rule in Saudi Arabia. In L. Blaydes, A. Hamzawy, & H. Sellam, eds., *Struggles for Political Change in the Arab World*, University of Michigan Press, pp. 102–23.

Herspring, D. (1987). Gorbachev and the Soviet Military. *Proceedings of the Academy of Political Science*, 36(4), 42–53.

Herz, J. (1952). The Problem of Successorship in Dictatorial Régimes: A Study in Comparative Law and Institutions. *Journal of Politics*, 14(1), 19–40.

Hinnebusch, R. A. (1983). From Nasir to Sadat: Elite Transformation in Egypt. *Journal of South Asian and Middle Eastern Studies*, 7(1), 24–49.

Hummel, S. (2020). Leader Age, Death, and Political Liberalization in Dictatorships. *The Journal of Politics*, 82(3), 981–95.

Huntington, S. (1965). Political Development and Political Decay. *World Politics*, 17(3), 386–430.

Hwang, I. (2006). The Third Handwritten Essay from a Former Core North Korean Official, the 'Frunze Academy Incident' and the 'Sixth Corps Incident' [전 북한 핵심 관료 육필수기 3탄 '프룬제 아카데미아 사건' 과 '6군단 사건']. *Shindonga*, March 3. https://shindonga.donga.com/3/all/13/105220/1.

Hwang, J. (1999). *I Saw the Truth of History* [나는 역사의 진리를 보았다], Hanul.

Hwang, J. (2006). *Memoirs* [회고록], Sidaejeongsin.

Hyun S. (2006). (The) Changes in the National Strategy and the Cadre Policies of North Korea [북한의 국가전략과 간부정책의 변화에 관한 연구], PhD Dissertation, Kyungnam University.

Ishiyama, J. (2014). Assessing the Leadership Transition in North Korea: Using Network Analysis of Field Inspections, 1997–2012. *Communist and Post-Communist Studies*, 47(2), 137–46.

Jeon, J. (2000). North Korean Leadership: Kim Jong Il's Balancing Act in the Ruling Circle. *Third World Quarterly*, 21(5), 761–79.

Jeon, M. (2009). The Kim Jong-il Regime's 'Military-first Politics': Structure and Strategy of Discourse. *The Review of Korean Studies*, 12(4), 181–204.

References

Jeong, G. (2019). North Korean Number 2 Choe Ryong Hae, How Did the Second Generation Partisan Bloodline Choe Ryong Hae Become North Korean Number Two [北 2인자 최룡해 빨치산 혈통 최룡해는 어떻게 2인자가 됐나]. *Wolgan Chosun*, 6.

Jeong, U. (2015). The Current State of North Korea's Energy Trade [북한의 에너지교역실태연구]. *Continued Research Reports*, 14–12, Korea Energy Economics Institute.

Jiang, J., Xi, T., & Xie, H. (2024). In the Shadows of Great Men: Retired Leaders and Informal Constraints. *British Journal of Political Science*, 1–27. doi.org/10.1017/S0007123424000012.

Jin, Q. (1999). *The Culture of Power: The Lin Biao Incident in the Cultural Revolution*, Stanford University Press.

Joffe, E. (1996). Party–Army Relations in China: Retrospect and Prospect. *The China Quarterly*, 146, 299–314.

Joo, S. (2012). North Korea under Kim Jong-un: The Beginning of the End of a Peculiar Dynasty. *Pacific Focus*, 27(1), 1–9.

Jung, C. (2000). *Kim Jong Il Seen Side On* [곁에서 본 김정일], Kimyeongsa.

Kandil, H. (2016). *The Power Triangle: Military, Security, and Politics in Regime Change*, Oxford University Press.

KCNA. (2013). Report on an Expanded Meeting of the Korean Workers' Party Central Committee Politburo [조선로동당 중앙위원회 정치국 확대회의에 관한 보도], *Korean Central News Agency*, December 9.

Kennedy, G. (2017). *From Independence to Revolution: Egypt's Islamists and the Contest for Power*, Oxford University Press.

Kim, H. (2015). *Dynasty: The Hereditary Succession Politics of North Korea*, Stanford University Press.

Kim, H., & Larson, J. (1988). Communication and Martial Law in the Republic of Korea, 1979–1988. *Canadian Journal of Communication*, 13(6), 87–91.

Kim, I. (2004). *The Complete Works of Kim Il Sung Volume 56*, Korean Workers' Party Press.

Kim, I. (2005). *The Complete Works of Kim Il Sung Volume 58*, Korean Workers' Party Press.

Kim, I. (2006). *The Complete Works of Kim Il Sung Volume 65*, Korean Workers' Party Press.

Kim, I. (2010). *The Complete Works of Kim Il Sung Volume 87*, Korean Workers' Party Press.

Kim, I., & Lee, M. (2009). Position-Shift Network of Power Elite and Regime Stability in North Korea [북한 권력 엘리트의 직위변동 구조와 정권의 안정성]. *North Korean Studies Review*, 13(2), 75–95.

Kim, I., & Lee, M. (2012). Predictors of Kim Jong-Il's On-the-Spot Guidance under Military-First Politics. *North Korean Review*, 8(1), 93–104.

Kim, J. (1997). We Are Falling into Anarchy Because of Food – Kim Jong Il's Speech to Commemorate the 50th Anniversary of Kim Il Sung University's Founding, December 1996 [우리 는 지금 식량 때문에 무정부 상태가 되고 있다 – 1996년 12월 김일성 종합대학 창립 50돌 기념 김정일의 연설문]. *Wolgan Chosun*, 4.

Kim, J. (2015). *The Collected Works of Kim Jong Il Expanded Edition Volume 25* [김정일선집증보판25권], Korean Workers' Party Press.

Kim, K. (2008). Changes in North Korea's Currency Exchange Control [북한의 외화관리시스템 변화연구], MA Dissertation: University of North Korean Studies.

Kim, K. (2009). The Change of Power Elites in the Kim Jong-Il Era [김정일 시대 권력엘리트 변화]. *Journal of Peace and Unification Studies*, 1(2), 103–39.

Kim, K. (2012). The Kim Jong-un Regime's Succession and Political Imperatives [김정은 정권의 출범과 정치적 과제]. *Unification Policy Studies*, 21(1), 1–24.

Kim, S., & Paek S. (2009). [Shocking Testimony] Former Spy From the 'Korean Workers' Party Office 35' Pak Kon-gil [says]: "From 1991 32 Soviet Nuclear Scholars Naturalized as North Koreans" [[충격증언] '조선노동당 중앙위원회 35호실' 출신 북한 고위공작원 朴健吉씨 "1991년부터 舊 소련 핵과학자 32명 북한에 귀화"]. *Wolgan Chosun*, 5.

Kim, T. (2015). The Study of North Korea's Control of Military Forces [북한 정권의 군부 통제 방식 연구], PhD Dissertation, Dongguk University.

Kim, T. (2021). Who Is Purged? Determinants of Elite Purges in North Korea. *Communist and Post-Communist Studies*, 54(3), 73–96.

Kirchgaessner, S., & Hopkins, N. (2019). Rumours Grow of Rift between Saudi King and Crown Prince. *The Guardian*, March 6. www.theguardian.com/world/2019/mar/05/fears-grow-of-rift-between-saudi-king-salman-and-crown-prince-mohammed-bin-salman.

Ko, J. (2007). A Study on the Characteristics of the Next North Korea's Military Officials [북한국의 차기 수뇌부 구성과 성격 연구]. *Journal of National Defense Studies [국방연구]*, 50(1), 111–46.

Koh, D. (2012). Vietnam: A Glass Half Full or Half Empty? *Southeast Asian Affairs*, 2012(1), 361–78.

Kokkonen, A., Møller, J., & Sundell, A. (2022). *The Politics of Succession: Forging Stable Monarchies in Europe, AD 1000–1800*, Oxford University Press.

Kokkonen, A., & Sundell, A. (2014). Delivering Stability: Primogeniture and Autocratic Survival in European Monarchies 1000–1800. *American Political Science Review*, 108(2), 438–53.

Koo, B., Choi, J., & Kim, J. (2016). Analyzing Kim Jong-Un's Survival Strategy from the Comparative Authoritarian Perspective. *Pacific Focus*, 31(2), 211–31.

Kou C., & Zang, X. (2013). Informal Politics Embedded in Institutional Contexts: Elite Politics in Contemporary China. In X. Kou & C. Zang, eds., *Choosing China's Leaders*, Routledge, pp. 1–21.

Kuhn, R. (2004). *The Man Who Changed China: The Life and Legacy of Jiang Zemin*, Crown.

Kurrild-Klitgaard, P. (2000). The Constitutional Economics of Autocratic Succession. *Public Choice*, 103(1/2), 63–84.

Kwak, M. (2018). *Research about Changes in the Functional Mechanisms of North Korea's Three Control Organizations* [북한 3대 통제기구 작동 메커니즘 변화 연구], Ministry of Unification.

Lachapelle, J., Levitsky, S., Way, L., & Casey, A. (2020). Social Revolution and Authoritarian Durability. *World Politics*, 72(4), 557–600.

Lam, W. (2006). *Chinese Politics in the Hu Jintao Era: New Leaders, New Challenges*, M. E. Sharpe.

Lankov, A. (2005). *Crisis in North Korea: The Failure of De-Stalinization, 1956*, University of Hawaii Press.

Lankov, A. (2013). *The Real North Korea: Life and Politics in the Failed Stalinist Utopia*, Oxford University Press.

Lankov, A. (2021). North Korea's Ruling Party Rule Revisions Presage Trouble at the Top. *NK News*, June 16. www.nknews.org/2021/06/north-koreas-ruling-party-rule-revisions-presage-trouble-at-the-top/.

Lawrence, C. (2020). Normalization by Other Means: Technological Infrastructure and Political Commitment in the North Korean Nuclear Crisis. *International Security*, 45(1), 9–50.

Leber, A., Carothers, C., & Reichert, M. (2023). When Can Dictators Go It Alone? Personalization and Oversight in Authoritarian Regimes. *Politics & Society*, 51(1), 66–107.

Lee, C. (1980). South Korea 1979: Confrontation, Assassination, and Transition. *Asian Survey*, 20(1), 63–76.

Lee, C. (1982). Evolution of the Korean Workers' Party and the Rise of Kim Chŏng-il. *Asian Survey*, 22(5), 434–48.

Lee, G. (2002). Characteristics of Kim Jong Il's On-the-spot Guidance. *Korean Institute of National Unification*. https://repo.kinu.or.kr/handle/2015.oak/652.

Lee, J. (1992). Kim Jong Il's Capacity to Rule [김정일의 통치력]. *Wolgan Mal*, 68, 82–93.

Lee, J. (1995). *Korean Workers' Party: Leadership Ideology and Structural Change* [조선로동당연구 – 지도사상과 구조 변화를 중심으로], Yeoksabipyeongsa.

Lee, J. (2000). *A New Understanding of Contemporary North Korea* [새로 쓴 현대북한의 이해], Yeoksabipyeongsa.

Lee, J. (2023). Research on KWP Politburo's Function and Nature under Kim Jong Il [김정일 시대 조선로동당 정치국의 기능과 성격 연구]. *National Strategy*, 29(4), 171–203.

Leverett, F. (2005). *Inheriting Syria: Bashar's Trial by Fire*, Rowman & Littlefield.

Mahdavi, P., & Ishiyama, J. (2020). Dynamics of the Inner Elite in Dictatorships: Evidence from North Korea. *Comparative Politics*, 52(2), 221–49.

Mahoney, J. (2004). Comparative-Historical Methodology. *Annual Review of Sociology*, 30, 81–101.

Mann, M. (1984). The Autonomous Power of the State: Its Origins, Mechanisms and Results. *European Journal of Sociology*, 25(2), 185–213.

Mansourov, A. (2013). Special Report: The Dramatic Fall of Jang Song Thaek. *38 North*, December 9. www.38north.org/2013/12/amansourov120913/.

Marcum, A., & Brown, J. (2016). Overthrowing the 'Loyalty Norm': Prevalence and Success of Coups in Small-Coalition Systems, 1950–1999. *Journal of Conflict Resolution*, 60(2), 256–82.

Matthews, A. (2022). Don't Turn Around, der Kommissar's in Town: Political Officers and Coups d'état in Authoritarian Regimes. *Journal of Peace Research*, 59(5), 663–78.

McDonell, S., Fraser, S., & Ng, K. (2023). Qin Gang: China Foreign Minister's Removal Sparks Speculation. *BBC*, July 26. www.bbc.com/news/world-asia-china-66299379.

McEachern, P. (2018). Comparative Authoritarian Institutionalism, Regime Evolution, and Stability in North Korea. *Asian Journal of Comparative Politics*, 3(4), 367–85.

McEachern, P. (2019). Centralizing North Korean Policymaking under Kim Jong Un. *Asian Perspective*, 43(1), 35–67.

Meng, A. (2020). *Constraining Dictatorship: From Personalized Rule to Institutionalized Regimes*, Cambridge University Press.

Meng, A. (2021). Winning the Game of Thrones: Leadership Succession in Modern Autocracies. *Journal of Conflict Resolution*, 65(5), 950–81.

MOU. (2011). *2011 North Korea's Who's Who of Officials in Organizations and Groups* [2011 북한 · 단체별 인명집], Ministry of Unification.

MOU. (2013). *2013 North Korean Who's Who of Officials in Organizations and Groups* [*2013* 북한 · 단체별 인명집], Ministry of Unification.

Mulvenon, J. (2001). *Soldiers of Fortune: The Rise and Fall of the Chinese Military-Business Complex, 1978–1998*, M. E. Sharpe.

Naughton, B. (2007). *The Chinese Economy: Transitions and Growth*, MIT Press.

O'Carroll, C., & Reddy, S. (2022). Reveal of Kim Jong Un's Daughter Sets Her Up as Successor: Ex-DPRK Officials. *NK News*, November 19. www.nknews.org/2022/11/reveal-of-kim-jong-uns-daughter-sets-her-up-as-successor-ex-dprk-officials/.

O'Donnell, G., & Schmitter, P. (1986). *Transitions from Authoritarian Rule: Tentative Conclusions About Uncertain Democracies*, Johns Hopkins University Press.

Oh, H. (2012). A Research on the Command System of North Korean Armed Forces in Kim Jong Il Regime [金正日時代 北韓 軍事指揮體系 研究], PhD Dissertation, University of North Korean Studies.

Olson, M. (1993). Dictatorship, Democracy, and Development. *American Political Science Review*, 87(3), 567–76.

Paek M. (2005). The Suspicious Death of Kim Yong Ryong, Embroiled in the History of the Ministry of State Security [보위사에 밀리던 김영룡, 의문의 죽음]. *Daily NK*, October 25. https://shorturl.at/rvCvH.

Panda, A. (2020). *Kim Jong Un and the Bomb: Survival and Deterrence in North Korea*, Oxford University Press.

Park, H. (2011). The Kim Jong Un Succession System, and Wholesale Replacements of Cadres in the Center and the Regions. *Korea Institute for National Unification*. https://repo.kinu.or.kr/bitstream/2015.oak/1895/1/0001447730.pdf.

Park H., Lee, K., Jung C., and Lee, G. (2004). *The North Korean Political System of the Kim Jong Il Era: Continuity and Change in Governing Ideology, Power Elite, and Power Structure* [김정일 시대 북한의 정치체제: 통치이데올로기, 권력엘리트, 권력구조의 지속성과 변화], Korean Institute for National Unification.

Park, Y. (2017). *The System and Function of the Workers' Party of Korea in Kim Jong-un Period: A Study on the Stabilization Strategy of Autocratic Regimes*, Korea Institute for National Unification.

Pepinsky, T. (2014). The Institutional Turn in Comparative Authoritarianism. *British Journal of Political Science*, 44(3), 631–53.

Quinlivan, J. (1999). Coup-Proofing: Its Practice and Consequences in the Middle East. *International Security*, 24(2), 131–65.

Ra, J. (2019). *Inside North Korea's Theocracy: The Rise and Sudden Fall of Jang Song-Thaek*, State University of New York Press.

Ri, J. (2012). *The Days Spent Strengthening Purity within the Revolutionary Ranks* [혁명대오의 순결성을 강화해나시는 나날에], Central Committee of the Korean Workers' Party.

Rodong Sinmun (2024). Great Socialist Wealth Born of Devoted Service for People's Wellbeing Respected Comrade Kim Jong Un Attends Commissioning Ceremony of Kangdong General Greenhouse Farm [위대한 위민헌신의 장정우에 솟아난 눈부신 사회주의재부 경애하는 김정은 동지께서 강동종합온실 준공 및 조업식에 참석하시였다], *Rodong Sinmun*, March 16. https://shorturl.at/Qvzi7.

Roessler, P. (2011). The Enemy Within: Personal Rule, Coups, and Civil War in Africa. *World Politics*, 63(2), 300–46.

Scalapino, R., & Lee C. (1972). *Communism in Korea: The Society*, University of California Press.

Schedler, A., & Hoffman, B. (2016). Communicating Authoritarian Elite Cohesion. *Democratization*, 23(1), 93–117.

Seawright, J., & Gerring, J. (2008). Case Selection Techniques in Case Study Research: A Menu of Qualitative and Quantitative Options. *Political Research Quarterly*, 61(2), 294–308.

Shambaugh, D. (2016). *China's Leaders: From Mao to Now*, John Wiley & Sons.

Shih, V. (2022). *Coalitions of the Weak*, Cambridge University Press.

Shih, V., Adolph, C., & Liu, M. (2012). Getting Ahead in the Communist Party: Explaining the Advancement of Central Committee Members in China. *American Political Science Review*, 106(1), 166–87.

Shim, S., & Tanenaka, K. (2011). North Korean Power-Behind-Throne Emerges as Neighbors Meet. *Reuters*, December 26. www.reuters.com/article/idUSTRE7BO02L/.

Shin, D. (2018). *Rationality in the North Korean Regime: Understanding the Kims' Strategy of Provocation*, Lexington Books.

Shin, D. (2020). *Kim Jong-Un's Strategy for Survival: A Method to Madness*, Rowman & Littlefield.

Sin, Y. (1996). *Until the Azalea Blooms, Part 1* [진달래꽃 필때까지 1], Munyedang.

Skidmore, T. E. (1989). *The Politics of Military Rule in Brazil, 1964–1985*, Oxford University Press.

Son, K. (2004). *Kim Jong Il Report* [김정일 리포트], Bada Books.

Song, W., & Wright, J. (2018). The North Korean Autocracy in Comparative Perspective. *Journal of East Asian Studies*, 18(2), 157–80.

Springborg, R. (1987). The President and the Field Marshal: Civil-Military Relations in Egypt Today. *MERIP Middle East Report*, 147, 5–42.

Springborg, R. (2018). *Mubarak's Egypt: Fragmentation of the Political Order*, Routledge.

Stenslie, S. (2016). Salman's Succession: Challenges to Stability in Saudi Arabia. *The Washington Quarterly*, 39(2), 117–38.

Stenslie, S. (2018). The End of Elite Unity and the Stability of Saudi Arabia. *The Washington Quarterly*, 41(1), 61–82.

Stenslie, S. (2020). Royal Succession in Saudi Arabia: The Rise of Mohammed bin Salman. In M. Kamrava, ed., *Routledge Handbook of Persian Gulf Politics*, Routledge, pp. 357–65.

Sudduth, J. (2017). Strategic Logic of Elite Purges in Dictatorships. *Comparative Political Studies*, 50(13), 1768–1801.

Svolik, M. (2012). *The Politics of Authoritarian Rule*, Cambridge University Press.

Szalontai, B. (2005). *Kim Il Sung in the Khrushchev Era: Soviet-DPRK Relations and the Roots of North Korean Despotism, 1953–1964*, Stanford University Press.

Talmadge, C. (2015). *The Dictator's Army: Battlefield Effectiveness in Authoritarian Regimes*, Cornell University Press.

Teiwes, F. (2000). The Problematic Quest for Stability: Reflections on Succession, Institutionalization, Governability, and Legitimacy in Post-Deng China. In H. Tien & Y. Chu, eds., *China Under Jiang Zemin*, Lynne Rienner, pp. 71–98.

Tertitskiy, F. (2018). 'Respected' Ri Sol Ju: A New Personality Cult for N. Korea's First Lady? *NK News*, April 16. www.nknews.org/2018/04/respected-ri-sol-ju-a-new-personality-cult-for-n-koreas-first-lady/.

Tertitskiy, F. (2022a). Evolution of the Institution of Political Officers in the North Korean Army: Coup-Proofing vs Military Effectiveness. *North Korean Review*, 18(1), 7–27.

Tertitskiy, F. (2022b). Kim Jong-il's Succession Campaign of the 1970s: A Comparison of Propaganda Tracks. *Acta Koreana*, 25(1), 29–52.

Tertitskiy, F. (2023). What the Titles of Kim Jong Un's Daughter Reveal About His Succession Plans. *NK News*, January 18. www.nknews.org/2023/01/what-the-titles-of-kim-jong-uns-daughter-reveal-about-his-succession-plans/.

Tertitskiy, F. (2024). *Soviet-North Korean Relations during the Cold War: Unruly Offspring*, Routledge.

Thae, Y. (2018). *The Third Floor Secretariat's Cypher: Thae Yong-Ho's Testimony* [3층 서기 실의 암호: 태영호 증언], Giparang.

Time. (1981). Sadat: A Faithful Pupil Takes Over. *Time*, October 19, https://content.time.com/time/subscriber/article/0,33009,924943,00.html.

Timoneda, J. (2020). Institutions as Signals: How Dictators Consolidate Power in Times of Crisis. *Comparative Politics*, 53(1), 49–68.

Timoneda, J., Escribà-Folch, A., & Chin, J. (2023). The Rush to Personalize: Power Concentration after Failed Coups in Dictatorships. *British Journal of Political Science*, 53(3), 878–901.

Torkunov, A., Toloraya, G., & Dyachkov, I. (2022). The Start of Kim Jong-Un's Era in North Korea: Political Consolidation. In A. Torkunov, G. Toloraya, & I. Dyachkov, eds., *Understanding Contemporary Korea from a Russian Perspective: Political and Economic Development since 2008*, Springer, pp. 25–37.

Wain, B. (2009). *Malaysian Maverick: Mahathir Mohamad in Turbulent Times*, Springer.

Wang, Y. (2022). *The Rise and Fall of Imperial China: The Social Origins of State Development*, Princeton University Press.

Ward, P. (2019). Purging 'Factionalist' Opposition to Kim Il Sung: The First Party Conference of the Korean Worker's Party in 1958. *European Journal of Korean Studies*, 18(2), 105–25.

Ward, P. (2020). The Structural Transformation of the North Korean Economic Planning System. In A. Buzo, ed., *Routledge Handbook of Contemporary North Korea*, Routledge, pp. 77–96.

Waterbury. J. (1983). *The Egypt of Nasser and Sadat: The Political Economy of Two Regimes*, Princeton University Press.

Weeks. J. (2008). Autocratic Audience Costs: Regime Type and Signaling Resolve. *International Organization*, 62(1), 35–64.

Willner, S. (2022). The Saudi Arabia of Mohammed bin Salman: Adapting to the Changing World and Preserving the Monarchy. *Israel Journal of Foreign Affairs*, 16(3), 365–78.

Wintrobe, R. (1998). *The Political Economy of Dictatorship*, Cambridge University Press.

Wit, J., Poneman, D., & Gallucci, R. (2004). *Going Critical: The First North Korean Nuclear Crisis*, Rowman & Littlefield.

Woldense, J. (2018). The Ruler's Game of Musical Chairs: Shuffling during the Reign of Ethiopia's Last Emperor. *Social Networks*, 52, 154–166.

Woldense, J. (2022). What Happens When Coups Fail? The Problem of Identifying and Weakening the Enemy Within. *Comparative Political Studies*, 55(7), 1236–65.

Woldense, J., & Kroeger, A. (2024). Elite Change without Regime Change: Authoritarian Persistence in Africa and the End of the Cold War. *American Political Science Review*, 118(1), 178–94.

Wong, S., & Chan, K. (2021). Determinants of Political Purges in Autocracies: Evidence from Ancient Chinese Dynasties. *Journal of Peace Research*, 58(3), 583–98.

Wright, J. (2021). The Latent Characteristics That Structure Autocratic Rule. *Political Science Research and Methods*, 9(1), 1–19.

Yi, D. (2003). *Why Doesn't North Korea's Military Coup? KJU Era Songun Politics and the Political Role of the Military* [북한 군부는 왜 쿠데타를 하지 않나], Hanul Akadaemi.

York, E. (2024). Ministries Matter: Technocrats and Regime Loyalty under Autocracy. *Political Science Research and Methods*, 12(1), 207–19.

Zwirko, C. (2021). Kim Jong Un Looks Thinner, and Intelligence Agencies Are Likely Paying Attention. *NK News*, June 8. www.nknews.org/2021/06/kim-jong-un-looks-thinner-and-intelligence-agencies-are-likely-paying-attention/.

Acknowledgments

Working on this Element has left us indebted to a large number of friends and scholars. However, the first group we would like to acknowledge will likely never read this Element: the North Korean people. Unlike many fantastic books and articles on North Korea, the North Korean people do not feature overtly in this Element. Instead, this Element is about how the Kim regime has survived, navigating the supposedly challenging hurdle of leadership succession on multiple occasions. Through leadership transitions, though, the Kim regime's brand of autocracy, and the atrocious human rights abuses that it has brought almost since the regime's inception, continues to endure. We therefore dedicate this Element to the North Korean people, in the hope that one day they can decide for themselves who their political leaders should be.

The ideas behind the Element were conceived during the early days of the Covid-19 pandemic. We are grateful to Jean Hong who supported the project, emotionally and intellectually, from an early stage. The University of York was kind enough to permit Goldring to abscond for six months for a fellowship at the University of California San Diego, where Stephan Haggard and Munseob Lee provided a welcoming community, as well as the invaluable commodity of time to help push the project forward. Stephan Haggard also generously provided funding to support a book workshop, for which we are extremely grateful. In Seoul, Andrei Lankov was also a kind supporter of the project, as was Cheong Seong Chang and various other scholars who we are unable to name here. In Vienna, Rüdiger Frank provided invaluable support that gave Ward the space and time to work on the project during his PhD.

Many others gave up their time to read parts of the Element and provide helpful and constructive feedback. We thank Quintin Beazer, Martin Dimitrov, Iza Ding, Charlotte Fitzek, Ken Gause, Chris Green, Sheena Chestnut Greitens, Mai Hassan, John Ishiyama, Holger Kern, Austin Matthews, Victor Shih, Fyodor Tertitskiy, Laron Williams, Ae Sil Woo, and Joseph Wright. We are also grateful to participants at numerous talks, including at the annual meetings of the European Political Science Association (2021), the Midwest Political Science Association (2021 and 2022), and the Western Political Science Association (2023), Empirical Political Science in Hong Kong (2021), the Woodrow Wilson Center and the National Committee on North Korea (2021), the Korean Political Studies Colloquium (2022), the University of California

San Diego (2023), the University of Edinburgh (2022), the University of Missouri (2022), the University of Strathclyde (2022), and the Virtual Workshop on Authoritarian Regimes (2022).

Parts of this Element have appeared in an article in *World Politics*. We thank the journal, its editors, the executive editor Emily Babson, and reviewers for supporting an overtly comparative project that focuses on North Korea, as well as providing constructive feedback that undoubtedly improved this broader project. We are also extremely grateful to the editors of the Cambridge University Press Elements series on Politics and Society in East Asia: Erin Aeran Chung, Mary Alice Haddad, and Benjamin L. Read. They provided insightful suggestions and were wonderful and extremely responsive editors for two early career researchers new to the world of Element publishing. We also thank a reviewer for the series whose feedback significantly improved the manuscript's overall presentation.

The Laboratory Program for Korean Studies, through the Ministry of Education of the Republic of Korea and Korean Studies Promotion Service of the Academy of Korean Studies, supported this work (AKS-2019-LAB-1250001). Goldring also acknowledges funding from the Korea Foundation (KF Ref. 1023000–1982).

Lastly, we would like to thank each other. Goldring thanks Ward for this encyclopedic knowledge of North Korea, his regular 'musings' (suggestions) about supposedly tangential theoretical ideas that could be integrated into the Element, and being an excellent dinner companion over 닭갈비 on the all too few occasions when we were able to work and socialize in person. Ward thanks Goldring for his systematic mind, ever-keen eye, and patience and kindness at every step of the way. We would also both like to thank our families, who are no doubt relieved to no longer have to listen to us talk about this project.

Cambridge Elements

Politics and Society in East Asia

Erin Aeran Chung
Johns Hopkins University

Erin Aeran Chung is the Charles D. Miller Professor of East Asian Politics in the Department of Political Science at the Johns Hopkins University. She specializes in East Asian political economy, migration and citizenship, and comparative racial politics. She is the author of *Immigration and Citizenship in Japan* (Cambridge, 2010, 2014; Japanese translation, Akashi Shoten, 2012) and *Immigrant Incorporation in East Asian Democracies* (Cambridge, 2020). Her research has been supported by grants from the Academy of Korean Studies, the Japan Foundation, the Japan Foundation Center for Global Partnership, the Social Science Research Council, and the American Council of Learned Societies.

Mary Alice Haddad
Wesleyan University

Mary Alice Haddad is the John E. Andrus Professor of Government, East Asian Studies, and Environmental Studies at Wesleyan University. Her research focuses on democracy, civil society, and environmental politics in East Asia as well as city diplomacy around the globe. A Fulbright and Harvard Academy scholar, Haddad is author of *Effective Advocacy: Lessons from East Asia's Environmentalists* (MIT, 2021), *Building Democracy in Japan* (Cambridge, 2012), and *Politics and Volunteering in Japan* (Cambridge, 2007), and co-editor of *Greening East Asia* (University of Washington, 2021), and *NIMBY is Beautiful* (Berghahn Books, 2015). She has published in journals such as *Comparative Political Studies, Democratization, Journal of Asian Studies*, and *Nonprofit and Voluntary Sector Quarterly*, with writing for the public appearing in the *Asahi Shimbun*, the *Hartford Courant*, and the *South China Morning Post*.

Benjamin L. Read
University of California, Santa Cruz

Benjamin L. Read is a professor of Politics at the University of California, Santa Cruz. His research has focused on local politics in China and Taiwan, and he also writes about issues and techniques in comparison and field research. He is author of *Roots of the State: Neighborhood Organization and Social Networks in Beijing and Taipei* (Stanford, 2012), coauthor of *Field Research in Political Science: Practices and Principles* (Cambridge, 2015), and co-editor of *Local Organizations and Urban Governance in East and Southeast Asia: Straddling State and Society* (Routledge, 2009). His work has appeared in journals such as *Comparative Political Studies, Comparative Politics*, the *Journal of Conflict Resolution*, the *China Journal*, the *China Quarterly*, and the *Washington Quarterly*, as well as several edited books.

About the Series

The Cambridge Elements series on Politics and Society in East Asia offers original, multidisciplinary contributions on enduring and emerging issues in the dynamic region of East Asia by leading scholars in the field. Suitable for general readers and specialists alike, these short, peer-reviewed volumes examine common challenges and patterns within the region while identifying key differences between countries. The series consists of two types of contributions: 1) authoritative field surveys of established concepts and themes that offer roadmaps for further research; and 2) new research on emerging issues that challenge conventional understandings of East Asian politics and society. Whether focusing on an individual country or spanning the region, the contributions in this series connect regional trends with points of theoretical debate in the social sciences and will stimulate productive interchanges among students, researchers, and practitioners alike.

Cambridge Elements

Politics and Society in East Asia

Elements in the Series

State, Society, and Markets in North Korea
Andrew Yeo

The Digital Transformation and Japan's Political Economy
Ulrike Schaede, Kay Shimizu

Japan as a Global Military Power: New Capabilities, Alliance Integration, Bilateralism-Plus
Christopher W. Hughes

State and Social Protests in China
Yongshun Cai, Chih-Jou Jay Chen

The State and Capitalism in China
Margaret Pearson, Meg Rithmire, Kellee Tsai

Political Selection in China: Rethinking Foundations and Findings
Melanie Manion

Environmental Politics in East Asia
Mary Alice Haddad

Politics of the North Korean Diaspora
Sheena Chestnut Greitens

The Adaptability of the Chinese Communist Party
Martin K. Dimitrov

Refugee Policies in East Asia
Petrice R. Flowers

The Welfare State in East Asia
Joseph Wong

Authoritarian Survival and Leadership Succession in North Korea and Beyond
Edward Goldring, Peter Ward

A full series listing is available at: www.cambridge.org/EPEA

www.ingramcontent.com/pod-product-compliance
Ingram Content Group UK Ltd.
Pitfield, Milton Keynes, MK11 3LW, UK
UKHW052321160225
455193UK00024BA/416